GCSE French

VOCABULARY

ABBEY HILL SCHOOL
KETTON ROAD
STOCKTON ON TEES
CLEVELAND TS19 8BU
TEL 01642 677113

Michael Buckby

Heinemann Educational Publishers, Halley Court, Jordan Hill, Oxford OX2 8EJ
A division of Reed Educational & Professional Publishing Limited

OXFORD   FLORENCE   PRAGUE   MADRID   ATHENS   MELBOURNE   AUCKLAND
KUALA LUMPUR   SINGAPORE   TOKYO   IBADAN   NAIROBI   KAMPALA   JOHANNESBURG
GABORONE   PORTSMOUTH NH (USA)   CHICAGO   MEXICO CITY   SAO PAOLO

First published 1996

00 99 98 97 96
10 9 8 7 6 5 4 3 2 1

A catalogue record is available for this book from the British Library on request.

ISBN 0 435 37859 7

Produced by Goodfellow & Egan

Photographs were provided by Michael Buckby

Printed and bound in Great Britain by Bath Press Ltd

CONTENTS

How to use this book   i

FOUNDATION TIER   1

A Everyday activities
Language of the classroom   1
School   4
Home life   8
Media   11
Health and fitness   13
Food   14
(For doctor, dentist and chemist
   see page 59.)

B Personal and social life
Self, family and friends   19
Free time, holidays and special
   occasions   20
Personal relationships and social
   activities   23
Arranging a meeting or activity   25
Leisure and Entertainment   26

C The world around us
Home town, local environment and
   customs   28
Finding the way   30
Shopping   32
Public services   35
Getting around   36
(For buying fuel, breakdowns and
   accidents see page 78.)

D The world of work
Further education and training   40
Careers and employment   40
Advertising and publicity   44
Communication   44

E The international world
Life in other countries and
   communities   46
Tourism   46
Accommodation   47
The wider world   50
(For youth hostels and campsites
   see page 88.)
Examination French   51

HIGHER TIER   54

A Everyday activities
Language of the classroom   54
School   54
Home life   56
Media   57
Health and fitness   59
Food   61

B Personal and social life
Self, family and friends   63
Free time, holidays and special
   occasions   65
Personal relationships and social
   activities   67
Arranging a meeting or activity   69
Leisure and entertainment   69

C The world around us
Home town, local environment and
   customs   71
Finding the way   73
Shopping   73
Public services   75
Getting around   77

D The world of work
Further education and training   80
Careers and employment   81
Advertising and publicity   83
Communication   83

E The international world
Life in other countries and
   communities   85
Tourism   86
Accommodation   88
The wider world   89

Solutions   90

◀ *How to use this book* ▶

This book contains all the words and phrases you need to learn in order to do well in your French exam. In some exams you may use a dictionary but if you know your key vocabulary and key phrases you will be able to work faster and complete all questions in the time available.

The words and phrases are presented topic by topic. There are two sections – Foundation and Higher. If you are taking GCSE Higher tier you should learn both sections. If you are taking GCSE Foundation tier you should concentrate on the Foundation section.

Verbs are given in the infinitive form.

Adjectives are usually given in the masculine form only. If the feminine form of the adjective is irregular it is given in brackets.

How to learn

Your learning will be much more effective and easy if you follow a few simple rules.

● Start several months before your exam: don't leave it to a last minute rush!

● Have regular and short learning sessions: three times 20 minutes each week is excellent, and better than one session of an hour.

● Before you begin a new topic, always go back and test yourself on the topics you have already learnt. In this way, you won't forget them.

● When you learn, it is essential to use your brain actively. Do not just sit and read the words: do things with the words which will help you to understand and remember them. The activities below can be used with any list. Try several of them with each list until you have learnt all the words in it.

Activities to help you learn

Learning the words

● Try to learn eight to ten words. Then cover the English and look at the French. Write the English equivalents and then compare what you have written with the book. Continue until you get them all right.

● Learn eight to ten words. Then cover the French and look at the English. Write the French equivalents and say the words to yourself as you write them. Then compare your list with the book. Continue until you get them all right.

● People tend to learn best the words at the start and finish of lists. To learn the words in the middle, re-write the lists and put the words in the middle at the top or bottom of your list.

● As you look at the list, write any words you are finding difficult to learn, omitting all the vowels (e.g. cahier – chr; ramasser – rmssr). Close your book and, looking only at your shorthand notes, write all the words in full.

- Make up a 'word-sun' as you look at a list. Write a key word in the middle and other words which relate to it at the end of each 'ray', e.g.

au bord de la mer

en avion

en été

nager

les vacances

quinze jours

passer

à l'étranger

jouer

Give yourself 30 seconds to 'photograph' this in your mind. Then cover up your 'word-sun' and try to write an exact copy of it. Compare it with the original.

Learning the sentences

- Try to learn six to eight sentences. Then write the first letter only of each word. Close your book and try to say, and then write, all the sentences in full. Check with the book and continue until you get them all right.

- As above, but writing just the first and last words of each sentence as your guide, plus the number of missing words. So, for 'Que veut dire ce mot?', you write Que ..... mot? (3).

- Copy any sentences in the list which are true for you or your school or town, etc. Then change the other sentences so that they are true for you. So, for example, if you think that tennis is the best game in the world, you would write 'le tennis' in the place of 'le cricket' in this sentence:

A mon avis, le meilleur sport du monde, c'est le cricket.

- Use a ruler to cover up parts of some sentences when you think you know them. Then see if you can fill in the gaps. You can cover sentences in different ways:

Vous aimez le boeuf?

j'adore les légumes.

Je déte___es oeufs

- For any sentences which you find hard to learn, write the English on one side of a small card or piece of paper, and the French on the other side. Keep these in a pocket or bag. Whenever you have a few minutes free, look at them in any order. If you see the English, say the French to yourself and then look at the other side and check. If you look first at the French, say the English to yourself and then check. Then shuffle the cards and do it again.

- You could make similar sets of cards, e.g.
  - Write a question on one side and the answer on the other.
  - Draw a picture on one side to illustrate the French sentence on the other side.
    Time yourself working on a set of cards and then try to improve on that time.

FOUNDATION TIER

EVERYDAY ACTIVITIES

◀ *Language of the classroom* ▶

Classroom instructions

apprendre	to learn		**absent**	absent
arrêter	to stop		**bravo**	great; well done
(se) corriger	to correct (oneself)		**c'est-à-dire**	that is to say
découper	to cut out		**compliqué**	complicated
demander	to ask		**difficile**	difficult
deviner	to guess		**exact**	correct
écrire	to write		**excellent**	excellent
entrer	to go in		**facile**	easy
essayer	to try		**fort**	strong; good
oublier	to forget		**lentement**	slowly
ouvrir	to open		**négatif(-ive)**	negative
répéter	to repeat		**trop**	too; too much
sortir	to go out		**vite**	quickly
souligner	to underline		**un exemple**	example
lève-toi	get up		**un livre**	book
levez-vous	get up		**une question**	question
venez ici	come here		**le silence**	silence
viens ici	come here			

Essayez de répéter avec un bon accent.	Try to repeat with a good accent.
Ouvrez vos livres.	Open your books.
Tu as oublié ton cahier?	Have you forgotten your exercise book?

Make classroom requests

excusez-moi	excuse me		**expliquer**	to explain
je m'excuse	I'm sorry		**excuser**	to excuse
s'il vous plaît	please		**s'excuser**	to apologise
un bic	biro		**fermer**	to close
un crayon	pencil		**montrer**	to show
une fenêtre	window		**perdre**	to lose
une gomme	rubber		**pouvoir**	to be able
une page	page		**prêter**	to lend
une règle	ruler		**trouver**	to find
les toilettes	toilet		**à**	to; at
aider	to help		**encore une fois**	once more
aller	to go		**quel**	which

Tu peux me prêter ta gomme?	Can you lend me your rubber?
Je m'excuse, j'ai perdu ma règle.	I'm sorry, I've lost my ruler.
Vous pouvez m'aider?	Can you help me?
Je peux aller aux toilettes?	Can I go to the toilet?

Say if you (don't) understand

comprendre	to understand		**pas**	not
non	no		**un peu**	little
oui	yes			

Tu comprends?	Do you understand?
Oui, j'ai compris.	Yes, I've understood.
Non, je n'ai pas compris cette phrase.	No, I didn't understand that sentence.

Ask someone to repeat

dire	to say		**une phrase**	sentence
entendre	to hear		**fort**	loudly
répéter	to repeat		**moins**	less
vouloir	to want		**pardon**	pardon
un mot	word			

Voulez-vous répéter la question?	Will you repeat the question?
Tu peux parler moins vite?	Could you speak less quickly?
Pardon, vous pouvez parler plus fort?	Sorry, could you speak louder?

Ask someone to spell a word

un accent	accent		**avec**	with
écrire	to write		**sur**	on

Ça s'écrit comment, s'il vous plaît?	How do you write that, please?
Avec un accent sur le 'e'?	With an accent on the 'e'?
Ça s'écrit avec deux 'r's.	It's written with two 'r's.

Here is the French alphabet with a guide to how the letters are pronounced:

A	Like <u>a</u> in bat.	**M**	Like <u>emm.</u>	**V**	Like <u>vay.</u>
B	Like <u>bay.</u>	**N**	Like <u>enn.</u>	**W**	Like <u>double vay.</u>
C	Like <u>say.</u>	**O**	Like <u>open.</u>	**X**	Like <u>eeks.</u>
D	Like <u>day.</u>	**P**	Like <u>pay.</u>	**Y**	Like <u>ee grec.</u>
E	Like <u>the.</u>	**Q**	Like <u>cupid.</u>	**Z**	Like <u>zed.</u>
F	Like <u>eff.</u>	**R**	Like <u>air.</u>		
G	Like <u>shay.</u>	**S**	Like <u>ess.</u>		
H	Like <u>ash.</u>	**T**	Like <u>tay.</u>		
I	Like <u>jeep.</u>	**U**	Like <u>duty.</u> (to say a		
J	Like <u>she.</u>		French 'u' make your		
K	Like <u>cap.</u>		lips round and try to		
L	Like <u>ell.</u>		say 'ee')		

Ask if someone speaks French or English

anglais	English		**parler**	to speak
français	French			

Vous parlez anglais?	Do you speak English?
Je préfère parler français.	I prefer to speak French.

Ask what things are called and what words mean

c'est	it is		quoi	what
comment	how		vouloir dire	to mean

Que veut dire cette phrase?	What does this sentence mean?
C'est quoi, en anglais/français?	What is it, in English/French?
Comment dit-on ça, en français?	How do you say that, in French?

Say you do not know

savoir	to know

Comment dit-on 'Je ne sais pas' en anglais?	How do you say 'I don't know' in English?
Je ne sais pas.	I don't know.

Say if something is correct

avoir raison	to be right		bien	well
avoir tort	to be wrong		correct	correct
corriger	to correct		faux(-sse)	false
faire	to make		juste	correct
travailler	to work		vrai	true
se tromper	to make a mistake		il y a	there is; there are
une erreur	mistake		quelques	some
une faute	error			

C'est correct?	Is that correct?
Il y a quelques fautes.	There are some mistakes.
Je me suis trompé.	I've made a mistake.
Oui, tu as raison.	Yes, you're right.

Une meilleure mémoire

Improve your memory!

With some practice it's actually possible to improve and develop your memory! A French psychologist, Monique le Poncin, has invented a method for doing this. It involves exercising all your intellectual faculties – a bit like fitness training! According to Monique le Poncin, nearly all people who have problems with remembering things simply need to improve their powers of concentration. The fact is, it's actually impossible to forget something. You may have problems locating a piece of information but it's there somewhere! So improving your memory involves getting better at finding what you're looking for, and finding it more quickly.

Here's what you do:

- First, identify the information you want to memorise and concentrate on it.
- Then, associate the information with as many different things and ideas as possible.
- Use a variety of strategies to help you memorise – e.g. visual memory (pictures, lists, colours, etc.) and audio memory (record words onto a cassette).

Just as with physical training you need to exercise regularly. To get the most out of your training follow these tips:

- Work in a quiet room.
- Work in the morning or at the end of the afternoon.
- Make sure you get enough sleep – your memory will perform better.
- Don't try to memorise after physical exercise or after a big meal.

The *Meilleure Mémoire* activities like the one on the following page will help you to train your memory. The important thing isn't getting the correct answer but doing the exercise!

Une meilleure mémoire 1

Activité visuelle

Regardez ces livres. Dites, le plus vite possible, combien de livres il y a.

Solution à la page 90.

◀ *School* ▶

Travel to and from school

une auto	car		**une station**	station
un autobus	bus		**aimer bien**	to quite like
une bicyclette	bicycle		**s'arrêter**	to stop
un bus	bus		**arriver**	to arrive
un car	coach		**partir**	to leave
le métro	the underground		**prendre**	to take
un vélo	bike		**quitter**	to leave
une voiture	car		**rentrer**	to return
un arrêt d'autobus	bus stop		**venir**	to come
un(e) camarade	school friend		**chez moi**	at home
de classe			**en**	by
un collège	secondary school		**d'habitude**	usually
une école	school		**en hiver**	in winter
une gare (routière)	(bus) station		**parce que**	because
une maison	house; home		**à pied**	on foot

Comment vas-tu au collège?	How do you go to school?
En hiver, je prends le bus.	In winter, I take the bus.
Ce matin, je suis venu à pied.	This morning, I came on foot.
Vous quittez la maison à quelle heure?	At what time do you leave home?
D'habitude, je pars à huit heures.	Usually, I leave at eight o'clock.
Je préfère venir en voiture parce que c'est plus rapide.	I prefer to come by car because it's faster.

When school begins and ends

l'après-midi	afternoon	moins	less
un cours	lesson	demi	half
une heure	hour	premier(-ière)	first
le matin	morning	quart	quarter
le soir	evening	troisième	third
commencer	to begin	après	after
finir	to finish	avant	before
terminer	to end	enfin	finally
dernier(-ière)	last	pendant	during
deuxième	second	vers	about

Les cours commencent à quelle heure?	At what time do the lessons begin?
Le premier cours commence à neuf heures et quart.	The first lesson starts at 9.15.
Les cours finissent à trois heures et demie.	Lessons end at 3.30.

Lessons: how many there are and how long they last

la biologie	biology	la technologie	technology
la chimie	chemistry	un emploi du temps	timetable
le dessin	art; drawing	un jour	day
l'éducation physique	physical education	une journée	day
l'EMT	technology	une leçon	lesson
l'EPS	physical education	une minute	minute
la géographie	geography	avoir	to have
l'histoire (f)	history	durer	to last
l'informatique (f)	information technology	assez	quite; enough
		à mon avis	in my opinion
les mathématiques (f)	mathematics	combien	how many
la musique	music	long(-ue)	long
la physique	physics	normalement	normally
la religion	religion	par	per
les sciences (f)	sciences	pas	not
le sport	sport		

Vous avez combien de cours?	How many lessons do you have?
Normalement, on a cinq ou six cours par jour.	Normally, we have five or six lessons per day.
Les cours durent combien de temps?	How long do lessons last?
Normalement, les cours durent cinquante minutes.	Normally lessons last 50 minutes.
À mon avis, c'est trop long.	In my opinion, it's too long.

Some important numbers:

dix	10	quarante	40	quatre-vingts	80
quinze	15	cinquante	50	quatre-vingt-dix	90
vingt-cinq	25	soixante	60	cent	100
trente	30	soixante-dix	70	mille	1000

Breaktimes and lunchtimes

la cantine	canteen		la récréation	play time; break
un copain	friend (male)		bavarder	to chat
une copine	friend (female)		jouer	to play
la cour	playground		manger	to eat
le déjeuner	lunch		rencontrer	to meet
le football	soccer		à midi	at midday; lunchtime
la pause de midi	midday break		en ville	in town

Le déjeuner est à quelle heure?	Lunch is at what time?
À midi dix.	At ten past 12.
Où manges-tu?	Where do you eat?
Je mange normalement à la cantine.	I normally eat in the canteen.
Que fais-tu pendant la pause de midi?	What do you do during the midday break?
Je bavarde avec mes copains.	I chat with my friends.
Il y a combien de récréations?	How many breaks are there?
Une le matin et une l'après-midi.	One in the morning and one in the afternoon.

Homework

une chambre	bedroom		utile	useful
une cuisine	kitchen		chaque	each
les devoirs	homework		dans	in
un frère	brother		faire	to do
une mère	mother		jamais	never
les parents	parents		longtemps	a long time
un père	father		mon, ma, mes	my
une soeur	sister		parfois	sometimes
beaucoup	a lot		souvent	often
ennuyeux(-se)	boring		ton, ta, tes	your
intéressant	interesting		très	very
inutile	useless		votre, vos	your

Nous avons trop de devoirs.	We have too much homework.
Je fais deux heures de devoirs par soir.	I do two hours of homework every evening.
Je fais mes devoirs dans ma chambre (dans la cuisine).	I do my homework in my bedroom (in the kitchen).

Extra-curricular activities

une activité	an activity		une disco(thèque)	disco
une boîte	nightclub		un échange	exchange
une carte postale	postcard		jouer aux échecs	to play chess
une cassette	cassette		un groupe	group
un championnat	championship		le jazz	jazz
un club	club		un match	match
un compact disc	compact disc		un membre	member
un concert	concert		la musique	music

le rock	rock music		**le tennis**	tennis
une semaine	week		**la voile**	sail; sailing
une soireé	evening		**adorer**	to love
le théâtre	theatre		**aimer**	to like
un timbre	stamp		**s'amuser**	to have fun
le week-end	weekend		**collectionner**	to collect
un centre sportif	sports centre		**danser**	to dance
l'équitation (f)	horse riding		**détester**	to hate
le hockey	hockey		**écouter**	to listen
la gymastique	gymnastics		**nager**	to swim
la lecture	reading		**casse-pieds**	annoying
la natation	swimming		**extra-scolaire**	extra-curricular
la pêche	fishing		**une fois**	once
la piscine	swimming pool		**puis**	then
le rugby	rugby		**sportif(-ive)**	sporty

Qu'est-ce qu'il y a comme activités extra-scolaires à ton collège?	What is there in the way of extra-curricular activities at your school?
J'aime écouter de la musique.	I like listening to music.
Hier soir, j'ai été à la disco.	Yesterday evening I went to the disco.
Ce soir, je vais aller au club de jazz.	This evening I'm going to go to the jazz club.

dimanche	Sunday		**jeudi**	Thursday
lundi	Monday		**vendredi**	Friday
mardi	Tuesday		**samedi**	Saturday
mercredi	Wednesday			

Une meilleure mémoire 2

Activité visuelle

Avant de faire cet exercice, révisez les pages 1 à 7.
Regardez ces vélos. Dites, le plus vite possible, combien de vélos il y a.

Solution à la page 90.

◀ *Home life* ▶

Jobs around the home

faire les courses	to do the shopping	la mère	mother
faire le lit	to make the bed	les parents	parents
faire le ménage	to do the housework	le père	father
faire la vaisselle	to do the washing-up	acheter	to buy
passer l'aspirateur	to hoover	avoir besoin de	to need
ranger	to tidy	débarrasser	to clear
nettoyer	to clean	laver	to wash
la cuisine	cooking	mettre	to put
la lessive	washing	nourrir	to feed
le jardinage	gardening	sortir	to go out; to put out
les affaires	things; belongings	travailler	to work
un aspirateur	vacuum cleaner	dans	in
une chambre	bedroom	ensuite	then
le fer à repasser	iron	une fois	a time
le jardin	garden	généralement	generally
la poubelle	dustbin	parfois	sometimes
une semaine	week	quelquefois	sometimes
la table	table	de temps en temps	from time to time

Que faites-vous pour aider à la maison?	What do you do to help at home?
Je passe l'aspirateur.	I do the hoovering.
Hier, j'ai fait la vaisselle.	Yesterday I did the washing-up.
Le week-end prochain, je vais faire du jardinage avec mon père.	Next weekend, I'm going to do the gardening with my father.

Your address and where you live

une adresse	address	un département	administrative division of France (like county)
un appartement	flat		
une avenue	avenue		
le code postal	post code	l'est	east
le centre	centre	le nord	north
un endroit	place	l'ouest	west
un étage	floor	le sud	south
une H.L.M	council house or flat	un pays	country
une maison	house	calme	quiet
un numéro	number	chez moi	at home
une place	square	en	in
un quartier	part of town	grand	big
une route	road	habiter	to live
une rue	street	moderne	modern
		petit	small
		vieux (vieille)	old

Où habitez-vous?	Where do you live?
J'habite à Hastings.	I live in Hastings.
C'est dans le sud de l'Angleterre.	It's in the south of England.
Tu habites une maison?	Do you live in a house?
Non, j'habite un petit appartement.	No, I live in a small flat.
Mon adresse, c'est le cent huit, rue de la Gare.	My address is 108, Station Street.

9

Some countries:

French	English		French	English
l'Europe (f)	Europe		le Danemark	Denmark
l'Angleterre (f)	England		la Norvège	Norway
l'Écosse (f)	Scotland		la Suède	Sweden
l'Irlande (f)	Ireland		la Finlande	Finland
l'Irlande du Nord (f)	Northern Ireland		la Grèce	Greece
le Pays de Galles	Wales		le Portugal	Portugal
la France	France		le Luxembourg	Luxembourg
l'Autriche (f)	Austria		les Pays-Bas	Holland
la Belgique	Belgium		la Suisse	Switzerland
l'Espagne (f)	Spain		les États-Unis (m)	The U.S.A.
l'Allemagne (f)	Germany		le Canada	Canada
l'Italie (f)	Italy			

Describe your home and its location

les Alpes (f)	the Alps		ancien(-ienne)	old
l'Atlantique (f)	the Atlantic		beau (belle)	good looking
un balcon	balcony		cher (chère)	expensive
la banlieue	outskirts		confortable	comfortable
un bâtiment	building		étroit	narrow
un bois	wood		joli	pretty
un bruit	noise		neuf(-ve)	new
la campagne	countryside		nouveau (nouvelle)	new
une cave	cellar		pratique	convenient
le centre-ville	town centre		typique	typical
une entrée	entrance		derrière	behind
un garage	garage		devant	in front of
un immeuble	building		donc	so
un jardin	garden		loin de	far from
le toit	roof		pas ... de	no
un village	village		près de	near to
une ville	town		presque	nearly
une vue	view		vraiment	really
affreux(-euse)	awful		aimer	to like
agréable	pleasant		louer	to rent

Parle-moi un peu de ta maison.	Talk to me a little about your house.
Elle est assez petite.	It's quite small.
Nous avons un garage et un jardin.	We have a garage and a garden.
On est près du centre-ville.	We're near the town centre.
C'est un quartier agréable et calme.	It's a pleasant and quiet part of town.

Your home: the rooms, garage and garden; their location, colour, size and contents

une cuisine	kitchen		un canapé	settee
une pièce	room		une chaise	chair
une salle à manger	dining room		une chose	thing
une salle de bains	bathroom		un escalier	stairs
une salle de séjour	living room		une étagère	shelf
un salon	lounge		un fauteuil	armchair
les WC	toilets		un frigidaire	fridge
une armoire	wardrobe		une lampe	lamp

un lavabo	washbasin		**un arbre**	tree
un lit	bed		**une fleur**	flower
les meubles	furniture		**une pelouse**	lawn
un miroir	mirror			
une moquette	fitted carpet		**blanc(-che)**	white
un mur	wall		**bleu**	blue
un oreiller	pillow		**brun**	brown
une photo	photo		**clair**	light
un piano	piano		**foncé**	dark
un placard	cupboard		**gris**	grey
le plafond	ceiling		**jaune**	yellow
une porte	door		**marron**	brown
un poster	poster		**noir**	black
un réveil	alarm clock		**orange**	orange
un rideau	curtain		**rose**	pink
un tapis	carpet		**rouge**	red
une chaîne-stéréo	stereo system		**vert**	green
un congélateur	freezer			
une cuisinière à gaz	gas cooker		**à côté de**	next to
un four	(microwave) oven		**en bas**	downstairs
(à micro-ondes)			**en haut**	upstairs
un frigo	fridge		**dehors**	outside
un lave-vaisselle	dishwasher		**en face de**	opposite
une machine à laver	washing machine		**en bois**	made of wood
un magnétophone	tape recorder		**en coton**	made of cotton
un magnétophone	cassette recorder		**électrique**	electric
à cassettes			**hi-fi**	hi-fi
un magnétoscope	video recorder		**en laine**	made of wool
une radio	radio		**en métal**	made of metal
un répondeur	answer-phone		**en plastique**	made of plastic
téléphonique			**plusieurs**	several
un téléphone	telephone		**sous**	under
une télévision	television			

Tu peux décrire ta maison?	Can you describe your house?
En bas, il y a la salle à manger, la cuisine et le salon.	Downstairs, there's the dining room, the kitchen and the lounge.
Dans ma chambre, il y a mon lit, une armoire et une chaise.	In my room, there is my bed, a wardrobe, and a chair.
Les murs sont blancs et bleus.	The walls are white and blue.

Taking a bath or shower

un bain	bath		**chaud**	hot
un bidet	bidet		**froid**	cold
une douche	shower		**heureusement**	fortunately
l'eau (f)	water		**malheureusement**	unfortunately
le savon	soap		**marcher**	to work
une serviette	towel			

Je peux prendre une douche, s'il vous plaît?	Please may I have a shower?
Malheureusement, la douche ne marche pas.	Unfortunately, the shower isn't working.

Needing soap, toothpaste or a towel

une brosse à dents	toothbrush		prêter	to lend
le dentifrice	toothpaste		s'il vous plaît	please (to an adult)
avoir besoin de	to need		s'il te plaît	please (to a friend)
donner	to give			

Tu as besoin de quelque chose?	Do you need anything?
Oui, je n'ai plus de savon.	Yes, I haven't got any soap left.
Tu peux me prêter du dentifrice, s'il te plaît?	Can you lend me some toothpaste, please?

Ask where rooms are

un escalier	flight of stairs		où	where
le rez-de-chaussée	ground floor		par ici	this way
les toilettes	toilet		par là	that way
à l'étage	upstairs		se trouver	to be
être	to be			

Où se trouve la salle de bains?	Where is the bathroom?
Elle est en haut, à côté de ta chambre.	It's upstairs, next to your bedroom.

Information about mealtimes

le déjeuner	lunch		l'heure	the time
le dîner	dinner		le petit déjeuner	breakfast
le goûter	afternoon snack for children		un repas	a meal

S'il te plaît, on mange à quelle heure?	At what time do we eat, please?
On prend le petit déjeuner vers sept heures et quart.	We have breakfast at about 7.15.

◀ *Media* ▶

Understand information about TV programmes, radio, music and performers

un acteur	actor		la télévision	television
une actrice	actress		une vedette	star
un chanteur	singer		il s'agit de	it's about
une chanteuse	female singer		célèbre	famous
un dessin animé	cartoon		classique	classical
un documentaire	documentary		drôle	funny
une émission	programme		extrêmement	extremely
un film d'amour	love film		formidable	great
un film d'aventures	adventure film		sensass	fantastic
un film policier	detective film		sous-titré	sub-titled
un film comique	comedy		terminer	to end
un film d'épouvante	horror film		en version française (originale)	in the French (original) version
les informations	news			
la musique pop	pop music			

Qu'est-ce qu'il y a à la télévision, ce soir?	What's on TV this evening?
Il y a un bon film comique.	There's a good comedy film.
Il y a une émission de musique pop.	There's a pop music programme.
Elle commence à neuf heures.	It starts at 9 o'clock.

Ask permission to use the telephone, radio, TV

allumer	to switch on		savoir	to know how to
écouter	to listen		téléphoner	to telephone
fermer	to switch off		un transistor	transistor radio
regarder	to watch			

Est-ce que je pourrais téléphoner à ma mère?	May I telephone my mother?
Excusez-moi, je peux regarder la télévision ce soir?	Please may I watch TV this evening?
Oui, tu peux l'allumer, si tu veux.	Yes, you may switch it on, if you want.

Films/programmes seen recently and music heard

un cinéma	cinema		hier	yesterday
une semaine	week		il y a ... (jours)	... (days) ago
un soir	evening		la semaine passée	last week
avant-hier	the day before yesterday		pendant	during
			(aller) voir	(to go and) see

J'ai vu un bon film samedi dernier.	I saw a good film last Saturday.
La semaine dernière, j'ai été à un concert.	Last week, I went to a concert.
Vous avez vu le dernier film de Depardieu?	Have you seen Depardieu's latest film?

Opinions about newspapers, magazines, TV, music

un article	article		mauvais	bad
un avis	opinion		moche	ugly; lousy
un jeu-vidéo	video game		négatif(-ve)	negative
un journal	newspaper		nul(-le)	no good
un magazine	magazine		passionnant	exciting
une opinion	opinion		pénible	painful
une pièce de théâtre	play		rire	to laugh
c'était	it was		super	super
amusant	funny		chanter	to sing
bon(-ne)	good		lire	to read
chouette	great		penser	to think
extraordinaire	extraordinary		préférer	to prefer
génial	terrific		mais	but
jeune	young		tout le monde	everyone
(pas) mal	(not) badly			

Tu as lu cet article dans ce magazine?	Have you read this article in this magazine?
Oui, il est très amusant, non?	Yes, it's very funny, isn't it?
Je ne lis pas le journal, parce que c'est ennuyeux.	I don't read the paper, because it's boring.

J'aime bien regarder la télé.	I really like watching TV.
Ce magazine est passionnant.	This magazine is exciting.
Le concert hier soir était nul.	The concert last night was no good at all.

Ask if someone agrees

d'accord	agreed		**il**	he; it
aussi	also		**moi**	me
elle	she; it		**si**	if
être	to be		**toi**	you

Tu es d'accord?	Do you agree?
Je suis d'accord avec toi.	I agree with you.
Qu'en penses-tu?	What do you think about it?

Une meilleure mémoire 3

Activité verbale

Avant de faire cet exercice, révisez les pages 1 à 13.
Dans chaque mot/expression, deux lettres sont absentes. Écrivez ces mots au complet, le plus vite possible.

1	un film d'ép_uva_te	6	une bros_e à d_nts
2	le p_tit déje_ner	7	un l_ve-va_sselle
3	l'A_lemagn_	8	un fa_te_il
4	le Ro_aume-Un_	9	co_fo_table
5	la s_lle à ma_ger	10	la na_ati_n

Solution à la page 90.

◀ *Health and fitness* ▶

How you feel

aller mieux	to be better		**ça va**	fine; O.K.
se coucher	to go to bed		**comme ci, comme ça**	not bad
dormir	to sleep		**fatigué**	tired
avoir faim	to be hungry		**mal**	badly
avoir soif	to be thirsty		**malade**	ill
se sentir	to feel		**pas mal**	not bad
bien	well		**peut-être**	perhaps

Comment ça va?	How are you?
Ça va bien, merci.	I'm fine, thanks.
Je me sens malade.	I feel ill.
Ça va mieux.	I'm feeling better.
J'ai chaud.	I'm hot.
Tu as faim?	Are you hungry?
J'avais très soif.	I was very thirsty.

Say where you have a pain

avoir mal à...	have a pain in ...		**le cou**	neck
un bras	arm		**une dent**	tooth
le coeur	heart		**un doigt**	finger

le dos	back		**le ventre**	stomach
l'estomac (m)	stomach		**les yeux (m)**	eyes
un genou	knee		**aïe!**	ouch!
la gorge	throat		**bouger**	to move
une jambe	leg		**être enrhumé**	to have a cold
une main	hand		**se faire mal**	to hurt oneself
le nez	nose		**ici**	here
un oeil (m)	eye		**là**	there
une oreille	ear		**lever**	to raise
un pied	foot		**un rhume**	a cold
la tête	head		**tomber**	to fall

Où est-ce que ça fait mal?	Where does it hurt?
J'ai mal à la tête (aux dents).	I've got a headache (toothache).
J'ai mal au dos (à l'estomac).	My back (stomach) hurts.
Je suis tombé.	I fell down.
Je me suis fait mal à la jambe.	I hurt my leg.
Ça fait mal ici.	It hurts here.

Call for help

attention	watch out		**méchant**	nasty; dangerous

Au secours!	Help!
Vous pouvez m'aider, s'il vous plaît?	Can you help me, please?
Attention! Le chien est méchant.	Watch out! The dog's dangerous.

Note: For consulting a doctor, dentist or chemist see pages 59–60.

◀ *Food* ▶

Opinions about food

le bifteck	beefsteak		**les frites (f)**	chips
le boeuf	beef		**un haricot vert**	French bean
un hamburger	hamburger		**la laitue**	lettuce
le jambon	ham		**un légume**	vegetable
le pâté	pâté		**un oignon**	onion
le poisson	fish		**une pomme de terre**	potato
le porc	pork		**une salade**	salad; lettuce
un poulet	chicken		**une tomate**	tomato
le salami	salami sausage		**la crème**	cream
une saucisse	sausage		**le fromage**	cheese
la viande	meat		**le lait**	milk
			un oeuf	egg
une baguette	French loaf		**un oeuf à la coque**	hard-boiled egg
les céréales	cereals			
les chips (m)	crisps		**un abricot**	apricot
un croissant	croissant		**une banane**	banana
les pâtes (f)	pasta		**un concombre**	cucumber
la pizza	pizza		**une cerise**	cherry
les spaghettis (m)	spaghetti		**une fraise**	strawberry
le toast	toast		**une framboise**	raspberry
			le fruit	fruit
une carotte	carrot		**une orange**	orange
un champignon	mushroom		**une pêche**	peach
un chou	cabbage			

une poire	pear		un plat	dish
une pomme	apple		la sauce	sauce; gravy
le raisin	grape		boire	to drink
			dommage	shame
un bonbon	sweet		nourrissant	nourishing
le chocolat	chocolate		rôti	roasted
la bière	beer		végétarien(-ne)	vegetarian
l'eau minérale (f)	mineral water			
le jus	juice			

Vous aimez le jambon?	Do you like ham?
Non, je suis végétarien(-ne).	No, I'm a vegetarian.
J'adore les légumes.	I love vegetables.
Je déteste le poisson.	I hate fish.
J'aime mieux le fromage.	I prefer cheese.
Je n'aime pas beaucoup le jus de tomate.	I don't like tomato juice very much.

Accept and decline food

un ananas	pineapple		bien sûr	of course
le chou-fleur	cauliflower		ça va comme ça	that's enough
une côtelette	chop; cutlet		délicieux(-se)	delicious
le gâteau	cake		désirer	to want
le potage	soup		encore	more
une poule	hen		et	and
le thé (au lait)	tea (with milk)		gentil	nice
			merci	(no) thank you

Vous voulez du chou-fleur?	Would you like some cauliflower?
Encore du potage?	Some more soup?
Oui, s'il vous plaît, avec plaisir.	Yes, please, with pleasure.
Merci, ça va bien comme ça.	No thank you, that's enough.
C'était délicieux mais j'ai assez mangé.	It was delicious but I've eaten enough.
Merci, j'ai déjà assez bu.	No thanks, I've already had enough to drink.

Testez-vous

How much does a cheese sandwich cost?

Ask for food and table items

le beurre	butter		un bol	bowl
un biscuit	biscuit		une cafetière	coffee-pot
la confiture	jam		un couteau	knife
l'huile(f)	oil		une cuiller	spoon
le miel	honey		(cuillère)	
la moutarde	mustard		une fourchette	fork
le pain	bread		une serviette	napkin;
le poivre	pepper			serviette
le sel	salt		une soucoupe	saucer
le sucre	sugar		une tasse	cup
le vinaigre	vinegar		un verre	glass
une assiette	plate		passer	to pass

Solution à la page 90.

Excusez-moi, mais je n'ai pas de verre.	Excuse me, but I haven't got a glass.
Passe-moi le pain, s'il te plaît.	Pass me the bread, please.
Vous avez du poivre, s'il vous plaît?	Do you have some pepper, please?

Call the waiter or waitress

| un garçon | a waiter | Mademoiselle | Miss |
| Madame | Madam | Monsieur | Sir |

| Monsieur/Madame, s'il vous plaît. | To attract the waiter's/waitress's attention. |
| La carte, s'il vous plaît. | The menu, please. |

Order a drink or simple meal

une boisson	drink	un chocolat chaud	hot chocolate
une bouteille	bottle	le coca (-cola)	coke
un café	coffee (black)	un jus de fruit	fruit juice
un café-crème	white coffee	au lait	with milk
la limonade	lemonade	le parfum	flavour
un orangina	orange drink	la pâtisserie	cakes; pastry
la carte	menu	le riz	rice
un citron	lemon	un sandwich	sandwich
une crêpe	pancake	un saucisson	slicing sausage
un croque-monsieur	toasted cheese and ham sandwich	la soupe	soup
		la vanille	vanilla
les crudités (f)	raw vegetables	le veau	veal
une entrecôte	steak	apporter	to bring
les fruits de mer (m)	seafood	choisir	to choose
le mouton	mutton	bien cuit	well done
une omelette	omelette	à point	medium (of meat)

Vous avez choisi?	Have you chosen?
Pour commencer, les fruits de mer.	To start with, the seafood.
Ensuite je voudrais du veau au riz.	Then I'd like veal with rice.
Comme dessert, je prendrai une crêpe au chocolat.	For dessert, I'll have a chocolate pancake.

Ask about availability / Ask for a fixed price menu

un dessert	dessert	le plat du jour	dish of the day
une entrée	first course	le plat principal	main course
une glace	an ice cream	un steak	steak
à la vanille	vanilla	inclus	included
à la fraise	strawberry	à prix fixe	fixed price
au chocolat	chocolate	recommander	to recommend
le lapin	rabbit	en sus	extra, in addition
le menu à cent francs	the 100 franc menu	le vin	wine
les petits pois (m)	peas	le yaourt	yoghurt

Vous avez des glaces?	Do you have any ice cream?
Qu'est-ce que vous avez comme fruits?	What sorts of fruits have you got?
Je prends le menu à cent dix francs.	I'll have the 110 franc menu.
Comme entrée, je prendrai les crudités.	For the first course, I'll have the raw vegetables.
La boisson est incluse dans le prix?	Is the drink included in the price?

Testez-vous

Le client, que dit-il?
A) Vous avez choisi?
B) Un café et un jus d'orange, s'il vous plaît.

C) Au secours!
D) Je peux prendre une douche?

Solution à la page 90.

Ask for an explanation

comme	like		**sans**	without
exactement	exactly		**une sorte de**	a sort of
manger	to eat		**une spécialité**	speciality
un pamplemousse	grapefruit			

Qu'est-ce que c'est exactement un croque-madame?	What exactly is 'un croque-madame'?
C'est un croque-monsieur avec un oeuf dessus.	It's a 'croque-monsieur' with an egg on top.
C'est chaud ou c'est froid?	Is it hot or cold?
C'est une sorte de poisson.	It's a sort of fish.
C'est comme une crêpe.	It's like a pancake.

Opinions about a meal

un plat	dish		**le service**	service
un repas	meal		**commander**	to order
un restaurant	restaurant		**mauvais**	bad
un serveur	waiter		**sauf**	except for
une serveuse	waitress		**tout**	all

C'était affreux.	It was awful.
Le service était excellent.	The service was excellent.
Les frites étaient froides.	The chips were cold.

Ask where the toilet or telephone is

une cabine téléphonique	phone booth		**à côté de**	next to
le couloir	corridor		**à droite**	on the right
le fond	end		**en bas**	downstairs
le sous-sol	basement		**en haut**	upstairs
le téléphone	telephone		**à gauche**	on the left
les toilettes	toilets		**là-bas**	down there
			près	near

Pardon, où se trouve le téléphone? — Excuse me, where is the telephone?
Au sous-sol, à côté des toilettes. — In the basement, next to the toilets.
Où sont les toilettes, s'il vous plaît? — Where is the toilet, please?

Ask for the bill

une addition	a bill		**une erreur**	a mistake
combien	how much		**le pourboire**	tip
compris	included			

Madame, l'addition, s'il vous plaît. — Excuse me, could I have the bill, please?
Il n'y a pas une erreur? — Isn't there a mistake?
Le service est compris? — Is the service included?

Une meilleure mémoire 4

Activité verbale

Avant de faire cet exercice, révisez les pages 1 à 18. Lisez ces mots. Qu'est-ce qu'ils ont en commun?
Ensuite essayez de les classer en quatre groupes.

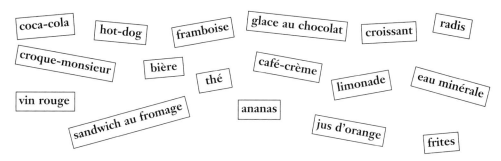

Solution à la page 90.

PERSONAL AND SOCIAL LIFE

◀ *Self, family and friends* ▶

Information about self, family, friends, pets

un ami	friend	un an	year
un beau-père	step-father	un anniversaire	birthday
un bébé	baby	une date	date
une belle-mère	step-mother	la Grande-Bretagne	Great Britain
un(e) camarade	friend	un mois (janvier,	a month
un(e) cousin(e)	cousin	février, etc.)	
un demi-frère	half-brother	s'appeler	to be called
une demi-soeur	half-sister	aimable	likeable
un enfant	child	bête	stupid
une famille	family	blond	blond
une femme	woman, wife	charmant	charming
une fille	daughter	les cheveux	hair
un fils	son	une couleur	colour
un garçon	boy	content	happy
une grand-mère	grandmother	court	short
un grand-parent	grandparent	dynamique	dynamic
un grand-père	grandfather	les lunettes (f)	spectacles
un homme	man	écossais	Scottish
maman	mum	égoïste	selfish
un mari	husband	gros(-se)	fat
un oncle	uncle	intelligent	intelligent
papa	dad	mince	thin
une tante	aunt	poli	polite
		roux(-sse)	red (hair)
un animal	animal	sérieux(-se)	serious
un chat	cat	sympa(thique)	nice
un cheval	horse	timide	shy
un chien	dog	triste	sad
un lapin	rabbit	gallois	Welsh
un oiseau	bird	en général	in general
un poisson	fish	irlandais	Irish
une souris	mouse	né le...	born on...
un cochon d'Inde	guinea pig	unique	only

Parle-moi un peu de ta famille.	Tell me a bit about your family.
J'habite avec ma mère et mon beau-père.	I live with my mother and step-father.
Tu as des frères et des soeurs?	Do you have any brothers or sisters?
Je suis enfant unique.	I'm an only child.
J'ai un chat qui est très drôle.	I have a cat who is very funny.

Spell your name, street and town

un nom	surname	la rue	street
un prénom	first name	la ville	town

Comment t'appelles-tu?	What's your name?
Ça s'écrit comment?	How is that spelt?
Quelle est votre adresse?	What's your address?

Testez-vous

Trouvez un seul mot pour compléter cette phrase:
Cette personne aime les ....

Solution à la page 90.

◀ *Free time, holidays and special occasions* ▶

Hobbies and interests

le basket	basket ball		**le volley**	volleyball
le cyclisme	cycling		**une boum**	party
une équipe	team		**une distraction**	leisure activity
faire des	to go walking		**un jeu**	game
promenades			**le loisir**	leisure
le handball	handball		**un ordinateur**	computer
faire du VTT	to go		**un passe-temps**	pastime
	mountain biking		**un roman**	novel
les patins à roulettes	roller skates		**une surprise-partie**	party
(m)			**gagner**	to win
les patins en ligne	roller blades		**jouer**	to play
(m)			**- aux cartes**	- cards
le ski	ski		**- de la musique**	- music
les sports d'hiver (m)	winter sports		**visiter**	to visit
un stade	stadium		**depuis**	since
un terrain	pitch; course		**préféré**	favourite
le Tour de France	the Tour of France			

Moi, j'aime beaucoup jouer de la guitare. Et toi?	I like very much playing the guitar. What about you?		
Mon sport préféré, c'est le volley.	My favourite sport is volleyball.		
Je suis membre d'une équipe.	I'm a member of a team.		
Je joue du piano depuis cinq ans.	I've been playing the piano for five years.		

Express simple opinions and agree or disagree with them

agréable	nice	**parce que**	because
beaucoup	a lot	**pourquoi**	why
moi non plus	me neither		

Tu as aimé le film?	Did you like the film?
Oui, c'était très intéressant.	Yes, it was very interesting.
À mon avis, c'était un bon match.	In my opinion, it was a good match.

Describe a recent holiday or leisure activity

une auberge de jeunesse	youth hostel	**au printemps**	in spring
une excursion	excursion	**quinze jours**	a fortnight
un lac	lake	**à Noël**	at Christmas
la mer	sea	**à Pâques**	at Easter
une montagne	mountain	**en avion**	by plane
une plage	beach	**au bord de la mer**	to the seaside
une région	region	**à l'étranger**	abroad
les vacances (f)	holidays	**en train**	by train
les grandes vacances	summer holidays	**faire des achats**	to go shopping
un village	village	**faire du camping**	to go camping
un séjour	stay	**passer**	to spend
en automne	in autumn	**rencontrer**	to meet
en été	in summer	**rentrer**	to return
en hiver	in winter	**rester**	to stay

Vous avez passé de bonnes vacances?	Did you have a good holiday?
Nous avons passé quinze jours en France.	We spent two weeks in France.
J'ai joué sur la plage.	I played on the beach.
Nous avons fait des excursions.	We went on some excursions.
À Pâques, nous sommes restés à la maison.	At Easter, we stayed at home.

Les mois	The months	**juillet, août**	July, August
janvier, février	January, February	**septembre, octobre**	September, October
mars, avril	March, April	**novembre, décembre**	November, December
mai, juin	May, June		

Preferences and alternatives for going out

le bowling	bowling alley	**un parc d'attractions**	theme park
un café	café	**la patinoire**	ice rink
un jardin public	park; public garden	**un spectacle**	show
un magasin	shop	**moi aussi**	me too
un musée	museum	**à partir de**	from
un parc	park	**sans eux/elles**	without them

Si on allait au café?	How about going to the café?
J'aimerais mieux aller à un concert.	I'd prefer to go to a concert.
Tu préfères aller au jardin public?	Do you prefer to go to the park?

Times and prices – buy tickets for leisure facilities

un adulte	adult		**une brochure**	brochure
un billet	ticket		**un bureau de**	
une entrée	ticket		**renseignements**	information office
une personne	person		**un jour férié**	public holiday
une place	seat		**un bal**	dance
le prix	price		**une piscine**	swimming pool
une réduction	reduction		**une salle**	room; cinema
une séance	performance		**un stade**	stadium
un ticket	ticket		**un terrain**	pitch; course
réduit	reduced		**cher**	expensive
coûter	to cost		**interdit**	forbidden
c'est combien?	how much is it?		**jusqu'à**	until
payer	to pay		**minuit**	midnight
réserver	to reserve		**ouvrir**	open

Le match commence à quelle heure?	What time does the match start?
Le concert finit à minuit.	The concert finishes at midnight.
Deux entrées pour la salle trois.	Two seats in cinema three.
Une personne, s'il vous plaît.	One person, please.

Pocket money

l'argent de poche (m)	pocket money		**donner**	to give
			gagner	to earn
un centime	one centime		**recevoir**	to receive
un franc	one franc		**un cadeau**	present
une livre sterling	one pound sterling		**les vêtements (m)**	clothes
mille	one thousand		**à court d'argent**	short of money
par mois	per month		**faire des économies**	to save money
dépenser	to spend			

Tu reçois combien d'argent de poche?	How much pocket money do you get?
J'ai quatre livres par semaine.	I get £4 per week.
Tu trouves que c'est assez?	Do you find that's enough?
Comment le dépenses-tu?	How do you spend it?
J'achète des vêtements.	I buy clothes.
Je travaille dans un magasin pour gagner de l'argent.	I work in a shop to earn some money.

◀ *Personal relationships and social activities* ▶

allô	hello (on telephone)	**bonsoir**	good evening
bonne année	Happy New Year	**enchanté**	pleased to meet you
bon anniversaire	Happy birthday	**joyeux Noël**	Happy Christmas
bon week-end	have a good weekend	**salut**	hi
bonjour	hello	**vous aussi**	you too

Bonne année!	Happy New Year!
Merci beaucoup.	Thanks very much.
Et toi.	You too.
Je te présente mon frère, Pierre.	This is my brother, Pierre.

(pas) bien	(not) good	**comment**	how
(pas) mal	(not) bad		

Bonjour, ça va?	Hello, how are you?
Comment allez-vous?	How are you?
Très bien, merci.	Very well thanks.
Et vous?	And you?
Toi aussi?	You too?

un ami proche	close friend	**membres de la**	members of the
connaître	to know	**famille (m)**	family
un(e)	penfriend	**présenter**	to introduce
correspondant(e)		**voici**	here is; this is
		voilà	there is; that is

Voici mon correspondant français, Michel.	This is my French penfriend, Michel.
Je te présente ma tante.	This is my aunt.
Tu connais déjà mon amie, Christine.	You already know my friend, Christine.

asseyez-vous	sit down	**donc**	then
assieds-toi	sit down	**entrer**	to come in

Entre donc.	Do come in.

Welcome a visitor

bienvenue	welcome		**à bientôt**	see you soon
bon voyage	good journey		**à demain**	see you tomorrow
bonne chance	good luck		**au revoir**	goodbye
bonne fête	good saint's day		**montrer**	to show
bonne nuit	good night			

Bienvenue chez nous.	Welcome to our house.
Tu as fait bon voyage?	Did you have a good journey?
Je vais te montrer ta chambre.	I'll show you your room.

Testez-vous

What time of year is it?
Solution à la page 90.

Thanks for hospitality

une année	year		**possible**	possible
l'hospitalité (f)	hospitality		**prochain**	next
une invitation	invitation		**remercier**	to thank
heureux(-euse)	happy		**revenir**	to return
merci	thank you			

Merci beaucoup pour votre hospitalité.	Thank you very much for your hospitality.
Vous avez été très gentils.	You've been very kind.
Je me suis très bien amusé(e).	I've had a lot of fun.

◀ *Arranging a meeting or activity* ▶

Suggestions for going out

une surprise	a surprise		**voir**	to see
une surprise-partie	a surprise party		**alors**	then
attendre	to wait		**car**	because; for
avoir lieu	to take place		**libre**	free
proposer	to suggest		**y**	there
sortir	to go out			

Tu veux venir à ma boum?	Do you want to come to my party?
Si on allait danser?	How about going to a dance?
On va faire une promenade?	Shall we go for a walk?
Tu es libre, demain soir?	Are you free tomorrow evening?

Inviting someone

après-demain	the day after tomorrow		**ce matin**	this morning
cet après-midi	this afternoon		**la pause de midi**	the midday break
demain	tomorrow		**inviter**	to invite
			demander	to ask

Je t'invite à ma boum lundi prochain.	I'm inviting you to my party next Monday.
Tu veux aller au match avec moi?	Do you want to go to the match with me?

Accept or decline an invitation

accepter	to accept		**désolé**	very sorry
accompagner	to accompany; to go with		**impossible**	impossible
décider	to decide		**maintenant**	now
devoir	to owe; to have to		**mieux**	better
il faut	it's necessary		**pendant que**	while
refuser	to refuse		**une raison**	reason
regretter	to regret		**si**	yes; if
ah, bon?	really?		**je veux bien**	with pleasure
certainement	certainly		**zut!**	damn!

Merci pour ton invitation.	Thank you for your invitation.
J'accepte avec plaisir.	I accept with pleasure.
Malheureusement, je ne pourrai pas venir.	Unfortunately, I won't be able to come.
Je regrette mais je dois rester à la maison.	I'm sorry but I have to stay at home.

Express pleasure

content	happy		**une idée**	idea
gentil(-le)	nice		**avec plaisir**	with pleasure

Ah, c'est gentil!	How nice!
Quelle bonne idée!	What a good idea!
Je suis très content(e).	I'm very happy.

Arrange a time and place to meet

à samedi (etc.)	see you on Saturday (etc.)	**devant**	in front of
ce soir	this evening	**à droite de**	to the right of
précis	precise, exact	**entendu**	O.K.
à quelle heure	at what time	**à gauche de**	to the left of
en retard	late	**prendre rendez-vous**	to arrange to meet
un arrêt	stop	**(se) rencontrer**	to meet (each other)
un rendez-vous	date	**se voir**	to see each other, to meet
derrière	behind		

À quelle heure est-ce qu'on se voit?	At what time shall we meet?
À midi, ça te va?	At midday, is that O.K. for you?
Où est-ce qu'on se rencontre?	Where shall we meet?
Je t'attendrai devant la disco.	I'll wait for you in front of the disco.

◀ *Leisure and Entertainment* ▶

Ask what is on at the cinema

aujourd'hui	today	**jouer**	to play
un film d'horreur	a horror film	**qu'est-ce que**	what

Qu'est-ce qu'on joue au cinéma aujourd'hui?	What's on at the cinema today?
Il y a un dessin animé?	Is there a cartoon?
C'est quelle sorte de film?	What sort of a film is it?

Find the cost of seats and buy tickets

une entrée	ticket	**une place**	seat
un(e) étudiant(e)	student	**une salle**	cinema screen
une personne	person	**une séance**	performance

La dernière séance commence à quelle heure?	At what time does the last performance begin?
C'est combien, s'il vous plaît?	How much is it, please?
Deux places pour la première séance, s'il vous plaît.	Two seats for the first performance, please.

Starting and finishing times

commencer	to start	**un spectacle**	show
finir	to finish	**tard**	late

Le film commence à quelle heure?	At what time does the film start?
Vers huit heures dix.	At about ten past eight.
Le concert finit à quelle heure?	At what time does the concert end?
Vers minuit.	At about midnight.

Opinions about events

amusant	amusing		c'était	it was
bien	well		nul(-le)	useless

Comment as-tu trouvé le film?	How did you find the film?
Tu as aimé le concert?	Did you like the concert?
C'était vraiment génial!	It was really terrific!
À mon avis, le spectacle était ennuyeux.	In my opinion, the show was boring.

Une meilleure mémoire 5

Votre mémoire immédiate

Avant de faire cet exercice, révisez les pages 19 à 27.
Observez cette grille pendant une minute. Puis fermez le livre et essayez de faire une grille identique mais en écrivant les noms des objets.

Solution à la page 90.

THE WORLD AROUND US

◀ *Home town, local environment and customs* ▶

Your home town and region

Douvres	Dover	**un fleuve**	river
Édimbourg	Edinburgh	**une forêt**	forest
Londres	London	**un mouton**	sheep
la Mer du Nord	the North Sea	**le paysage**	countryside
une bibliothèque	library	**une rivière**	river
un camping	campsite	**une vache**	cow
une cathédrale	cathedral	**au bord de la mer**	seaside
un château	castle	**une distraction**	leisure activity
une église	church	**un habitant**	inhabitant
une ferme	farm	**un kilomètre**	kilometre
un hôtel de ville	town hall	**un million de**	million
une mairie	town hall	**une région**	region
un monument	monument	**calme**	quiet
une place	square	**entre**	between
un pont	bridge	**historique**	historical
un port	port	**touristique**	tourist
un bois	wood	**important**	big; important
la campagne	countryside	**industriel(-le)**	industrial
un champ	field	**loin de**	far from
la colline	hill	**proche**	nearby, close
la côte	coast	**rien**	nothing
une fleur	flower	**situé**	situated

Qu'est-ce qu'il y a à voir?	What is there to see?
Il y a un vieux château.	There's an old castle.
C'est une ville industrielle dans l'ouest de l'Écosse.	It's an industrial town in the west of Scotland.
La région est belle.	The region is beautiful.

Show a visitor around your town

descendre	to go down	**regarder**	to look
intéresser	to interest	**tout droit**	straight on
monter	to go up	**tout près**	nearby

Vous voulez visiter la ville?	Would you like to look round the town?
Voilà notre mairie.	That's our town hall.
Descendez cette rue et tournez à gauche.	Go down this street and turn left.

Travelling into town

en auto	by car	la gare (SNCF)	the (railway) station
à vélo	by bicycle	quitter	to leave
en train	by train	un taxi	taxi
en voiture	by car	le temps	time

Pour aller en ville, on prend le métro?	To go into town, do we take the underground?
Il y a un bus tous les combien?	How often is there a bus?
Toutes les vingt minutes.	Every 20 minutes.
Ça prend combien de temps?	How long does it take?
Quinze minutes environ.	About 15 minutes.

Important festivals

un anniversaire	birthday	religieux(ieuse)	religious
une carte	card	spécial	special
une fête	holiday; festival		
le Noël	Christmas	le premier janvier	the 1st of January
le Nouvel An	New Year	le premier mai	the 1st of May
les Pâques	Easter	le quatorze juillet	the 14th of July
la religion	religion	le onze novembre	the 11th of November
avoir lieu	to take place		
se passer	to happen	le vingt-cinq décembre	the 25th of December
important	important		

Pour toi, la fête la plus importante, c'est quand?	When is the most important festival for you?
Moi, j'adore mon anniversaire.	I love my birthday.
On m'envoie beaucoup de cartes.	People send me a lot of cards.
Je reçois des cadeaux.	I receive presents.
Toute la famille reste à la maison.	All the family stays at home.

Understand weather forecasts

le climat	climate	la température	temperature
demain	tomorrow	la Bretagne	Britanny
plus tard	later	la Manche	the English Channel
la météo	weather forecast	le Massif Central	the Massif Central in France
les prévisions (f)	forecasts		
le temps	weather	la Méditerranée	the Mediterranean sea
l'après-midi (m)	afternoon		
le matin	morning	le Midi	the south of France
la nuit	night	Montréal	Montreal
le soir	evening	la Normandie	Normandy
un degré	degree	parisien(-ne)	Parisian
la glace	ice	agréable	pleasant
un nuage	cloud	beau (belle)	fine
la pluie	rain	chaud	hot

compliqué	complicated	**rare**	rare
fort	strong	**après**	after
froid	cold	**avant**	before
geler	to freeze	**pendant**	during
léger(-ère)	light	**quelquefois**	sometimes
mauvais	bad	**rapidement**	quickly
meilleur	best	**souvent**	often

Quel temps fera-t-il demain?	What will the weather be like tomorrow?
D'après la météo, il y aura des nuages.	According to the forecast, there will be clouds.
Le matin, il fera beau.	In the morning, the weather will be fine.
On dit qu'il fera chaud.	They say it will be hot.

Understand and describe weather conditions

le brouillard	fog	**pleuvoir**	to rain
un éclair	flash of lightning	**Bruxelles**	Brussels
la neige	snow	**la Garonne**	the river Garonne
le soleil	sun	**la Loire**	the river Loire
le vent	wind	**les Pyrénées**	the Pyrenees
faible	weak	**le Québec**	Quebec
mouillé	wet	**le Rhône**	the river Rhone
briller	to shine	**la Seine**	the river Seine
neiger	to snow	**en même temps**	at the same time

Quel mauvais temps!	What awful weather!
Il y a du vent.	It's windy.
Normalement, il fait beau en été.	Normally, the weather is good in summer.
Il a neigé toute la nuit.	It snowed all night.

◀ *Finding the way* ▶

Attracting the attention of a passer-by

Madame	Madam	**Monsieur**	Sir
Mademoiselle	Miss	**pardon**	excuse me

Pardon, madame.	What you say to attract the attention of a woman.
Pardon, mademoiselle.	What you say to attract the attention of a girl.

How to get to a place

une carte	map	**une autoroute**	motorway
les directions	directions	**une banque**	bank
la distance	distance	**un carrefour**	crossroads
un office de tourisme	tourist office	**un coin**	corner
un plan	town plan	**un commissariat**	police station
un syndicat d'initiative	tourist information office	**un feu rouge**	traffic light
		un hôpital	hospital

la RN10	the RN10 road		**là-bas**	down there
la poste	post office		**toutes directions**	all directions
un rond-point	roundabout		**continuer**	to continue
une route	road		**tourner**	to turn
au bout de	at the end of		**descendre**	to go down
enfin	finally		**passer**	to cross, to pass
ensuite	then		**traverser**	to cross
en face de	opposite			

Il y a une poste près d'ici?	Is there a post office near here?
Allez tout droit et passez le pont.	Go straight on and cross the bridge.
Vous allez jusqu'à l'hôpital où vous tournez à gauche.	Go as far as the hospital where you turn left.
Pour aller au château, s'il vous plaît?	How do I get to the castle, please?
Prenez la première rue à droite.	Take the first street on the right.
C'est juste après le rond-point.	It's just after the roundabout.
La banque est en face de la mairie.	The bank is opposite the town hall.

Testez-vous

Choisissez la meilleure réponse à cette question:
Pardon, pour aller à la cathédrale, s'il vous plaît?
Solution à la page 90.

Nearby or far away?

à ... kilomètres de	... kilometres from		**un magasin d'alimentation**	food shop
à ... mètres	... metres away		**autre**	other
à ... minutes	... minutes away		**loin (d'ici)**	far (from here)
une confiserie	sweet shop		**ou**	or
			près (d'ici)	near (here)

La gare routière est loin d'ici?	Is the bus station far from here?
Non, elle est tout près.	No, it's quite close.
Il y a un autre hôtel près d'ici?	Is there another hotel near here?
Il y en a un à trois kilomètres.	There is one three kilometres away.
L'autoroute est à dix minutes d'ici.	The motorway is ten minutes from here.
Il y a une confiserie au coin de la rue.	There is a sweet shop on the corner of the street.

Thanks

merci (beaucoup)	thank you (very much)	**de rien**	don't mention it
		il n'y a pas de quoi	not at all

Merci beaucoup, monsieur.	Thank you very much, sir.
De rien, madame.	Don't mention it, madam.

◀ *Shopping* ▶

Finding shops and supermarkets

une boucherie	butcher's	**une librairie**	bookshop
une boulangerie	baker's	**un grand magasin**	department store
une boutique	shop	**un marché**	market
un bureau de tabac	tobacconist's	**une parfumerie**	perfume shop
un centre commercial	shopping centre	**une pâtisserie**	cake shop
une charcuterie	pork butcher's	**une pharmacie**	chemist's
une épicerie	grocer's	**une poissonnerie**	fish shop
un hypermarché	hypermarket	**un supermarché**	supermarket
		chercher	to look for

Où est la boulangerie?	Where is the baker's?
Il y a un centre commercial ici?	Is there a shopping centre here?
Où se trouve le supermarché le plus proche?	Where is the closest supermarket?

Opening and closing times

fermé	closed	**entre**	between
ouvert	open	**fermer**	to close

La banque ouvre à quelle heure?	At what time does the bank open?
Le magasin est ouvert jusqu'à midi.	The shop is open until midday.
Vous fermez à quelle heure?	At what time do you close?
On est fermé entre midi et quart et une heure et demie.	We're closed between 12.15 and 1.30.

Testez-vous

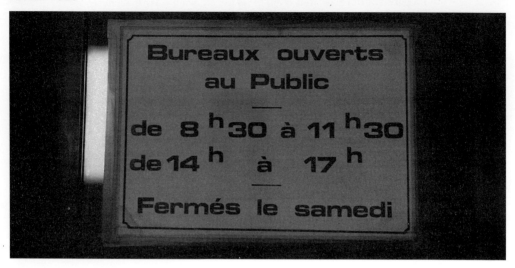

When are these offices closed?
Solution à la page 90.

Colour, size, who an item is for

un anorak	anorak	le cuir	leather
des baskets	trainers	la laine	wool
un chapeau	hat	le nylon	nylon
une chaussette	sock	la mode	fashion
une chaussure	shoe	une liste	list
une chemise	shirt	gris	grey
un chemisier	blouse	jaune	yellow
un collant	pair of tights	même	same
une cravate	tie	violet(-tte)	violet
un gant	glove	il n'y en a pas	there aren't any
un imperméable	mac	un disque	record
un jean	pair of jeans	une enveloppe	envelope
une jupe	skirt	un mouchoir	handkerchief
un maillot de bain	swim suit	un parapluie	umbrella
un manteau	coat	le parfum	perfume
une paire de	a pair of	un sac	bag
un pantalon	pair of trousers	l'argent	money
un pull(over)	pullover	la caisse	cash desk
un pyjama	pair of pyjamas	gratuit	free
une robe	dress	la monnaie	change
une sandale	sandal	les soldes	sale
un short	pair of shorts	large	wide
un slip	underpants	léger(-ère)	light
un soutien-gorge	bra	lourd	heavy
un T-shirt	Tee-shirt	moyen(-ne)	medium
une veste	jacket	la pointure	size (for shoes)
les vêtements	clothes	une taille	size (for clothes)
le coton	cotton		

Je voudrais une paire de chaussettes.	I'd like a pair of socks.
Pointure quarante-quatre.	Size 44.
Avez-vous cet imperméable en rouge?	Have you got this mac in red?
Quelle taille?	What size?
Moyenne.	Medium.
Je dois acheter du parfum pour ma mère.	I must buy some perfume for my mother.

Weight, volume, container

une boîte	box; tin		**un gramme**	gram
une bouteille	bottle		**un kilo**	kilo
une douzaine	dozen		**un litre**	litre
un morceau	a bit		**une livre**	pound
un paquet	packet		**ça va comme ça**	that's fine
un peu	a little		**combien**	how much, many
un pot	jar		**beaucoup**	a lot
un sac	bag		**plus petit**	smaller
une tranche	slice		**la crème Chantilly**	whipped cream
un verre	glass		**le papier**	paper

Je voudrais un kilo de poires.	I'd like a kilo of pears.
Donnez-moi aussi une bouteille d'orangina.	Give me a bottle of orangeade as well.
Je peux avoir un morceau de ce fromage?	Can I have a piece of that cheese?
Comme ça?	Like that?
Non, un peu moins grand.	No, a little smaller.

Non-availability; answer 'Is that all?'

avec ça	with that		**ne ... plus**	no more
c'est tout	that's all		**ne ... rien**	nothing
il n'y en a pas	there isn't (aren't) any		**pas (de)**	no
			un peu plus	a little more
ne ... aucun	no, none			

Il n'y a plus de chips.	There are no crisps left.
C'est tout?	Is that all?
Ce sera tout, merci.	That will be all, thank you.
Donnez-moi aussi une boîte de petits pois.	Give me a tin of peas as well.

Opinions about clothes

beau (belle)	good looking		**à la mode**	fashionable
bon marché	inexpensive		**bof!**	so what!
différent	different		**coûter**	to cost

Tu aimes mon maillot de bain?	Do you like my swimsuit?
Il est très joli.	It's very pretty.
Cette robe est belle, n'est-ce pas?	That dress is beautiful isn't it?
Je préfère celle-là.	I prefer that one.

Testez-vous

ARCADIA KLEBER
① CLAIRE BARRAT
   Prêt à Porter Féminin
② TEMPO DUE
   Prêt à Porter Masculin
③ DIVA
   Prêt à Porter Féminin
④ SERENISSIME
   Bijouterie
⑤ J.LOUIS DAVID
   Coiffure
⑥ LEONE RESTAURANT
   Cuisine Lyonnaise - Salon de Thé
⑦ L'HOMME cet Univers
   Parfumerie
⑧ TAPIS D'ORIENT
⑨ LINEAO
   Chausseur-Ensemblier

Qu'est-ce qu'on peut acheter à la boutique
numéro deux?
Solution à la page 90.

Buying something or not

court	short
long	long
devoir	to have to; to owe
merci	(no) thank you

D'accord, je prends ce pantalon.	Fine, I'll take this pair of trousers.
Ce short est trop cher.	These shorts are too expensive.
Vous avez quelque chose de moins cher?	Do you have anything less expensive?
Je vous dois combien?	How much do I owe you?

◀ *Public services* ▶

Ask where a post office, 'tabac' or letter box is

une boîte aux lettres	letter box
un bureau de poste	post office
les P. et T. (f)	post office

un tabac	tobacconist's
près d'ici	near here
se trouver	to be

Où est la poste?	Where is the post office?
Il y a une boîte aux lettres près d'ici?	Is there a letter box near here?
Il y en a une en face du tabac.	There is one opposite the tobacconist's.

Sending a letter or postcard home

en Angleterre	to England
en Écosse	to Scotland
en Grande-Bretagne	to Great Britain
en Irlande	to Ireland
en Irlande du Nord	to Northern Ireland
au Pays de Galles	to Wales

au Royaume-Uni	to the U.K.
une carte postale	postcard
une lettre	letter
par avion	by air
envoyer	to send

Je voudrais envoyer une lettre en Grande-Bretagne.	I'd like to send a letter to Great Britain.
C'est combien pour envoyer une carte postale au Royaume-Uni?	How much is it to send a postcard to the U.K?

Ask for stamps / Finding a telephone

une cabine téléphonique	phone box	**un timbre**	stamp
un centime	centime	**un timbre à un franc (etc.)**	one franc stamp
un téléphone public	public telephone	**donner**	to give

Un timbre à deux francs quatre-vingts, s'il vous plaît.	A two franc, 80 centimes stamp, please.
Y a-t-il un téléphone public près d'ici?	Is there a public 'phone near here?
Il y a une cabine téléphonique en face de la poste.	There's a 'phone box opposite the post office.

◀ *Getting around* ▶

How to get into town

un (auto) car	coach	**il faut**	it is necessary
un dépliant	leaflet	**quelquefois**	sometimes
une station de métro	underground station	**rapide**	fast
une place	seat	**voyager**	to travel
changer	to change		

Comment peut-on aller au centre-ville?	How can one get into the town centre?
On pourrait prendre le métro.	We could take the underground.
C'est direct?	Is it direct?
Non, il faut changer.	No, you must change.

Signs and notices

le buffet	station buffet	**la direction**	direction
une consigne (automatique)	(automatic) luggage office	**la douane**	customs
le guichet	ticket office	**eau potable**	drinking water
un horaire	timetable	**eau non potable**	water not for drinking
les objets trouvés	lost property	**une entrée**	entrance
un quai	platform	**un express**	express
les renseignements (m)	information	**un voyageur**	traveller
la réservation	reservation	**assis**	sitting
la salle d'attente	waiting room	**composter**	to date-stamp
la sortie	exit	**debout**	standing
la sortie de secours	emergency exit	**défense de fumer**	no smoking
la voie	platform	**(non-) fumeur**	(non) smoking
l'arrivée (f)	arrival	**occupé**	occupied, engaged
les bagages	luggage	**poussez**	push
une correspondance	connection	**en provenance de**	from
le départ	departure	**en retard**	late
la destination	destination	**tirez**	pull

Le train à destination de Bordeaux part dans cinq minutes.
Attention! Le train en provenance de Strasbourg arrivera en gare dans deux minutes, avec huit minutes de retard.

The train to Bordeaux leaves in five minutes.
Attention! The train from Strasbourg will arrive at the station in two minutes, eight minutes late.

Testez-vous

You see this in France. Your parents ask you what the sign means. Tell them.

Solution à la page 90.

Getting to a particular place

Bruxelles	Brussels
un (auto) bus	bus
un numéro	number
un train	train
s'arrêter	to stop
qui	who; which

Pardon, il y a un car qui va à Boulogne?	Excuse me, is there a coach which goes to Boulogne?
Cet autobus s'arrête à la gare SNCF?	Does this bus stop at the railway station?
C'est quel numéro pour aller à la plage?	Which number is it to go to the beach?

Some important French towns

Bordeaux	Boulogne	Calais	Cherbourg
Dieppe	le Havre	Lyon	Marseille
Paris	Strasbourg		

Find bus stops, toilets and platforms

un arrêt	stop		**les toilettes**	toilets
un quai	platform		**une voie**	platform

Y a-t-il un arrêt d'autobus près d'ici?	Is there a bus stop near here?
Oui, il est en face du collège.	Yes, it's opposite the school.
Où sont les toilettes?	Where are the toilets?
Le train pour Lyon part de quel quai?	Which platform does the Lyon train leave from?

Buying tickets

un aller-retour	return		une classe	class
un aller-simple	single		un ticket	ticket
un billet	ticket		fumeur	smoking
un carnet	book of tickets		non-fumeur	non-smoking

Un aller-retour pour Lyon, s'il vous plaît.	A return ticket to Lyon, please.
En quelle classe?	Which class?
Deuxième classe.	Second class.

Times of arrival and departure

attendre	to wait		partir	to leave
arriver	to arrive		un retard	delay
au moins	at least			

Le train pour Lyon part à quelle heure?	At what time does the train for Lyon leave?
L'express pour le Havre part à quinze heures vingt-cinq.	The express for le Havre leaves at 15.25.
Le car arrive à Bruxelles à quelle heure?	At what time does the coach arrive in Brussels?

Ticket checks

contrôler	to check		perdre	to lose
montrer	to show			

Votre billet, s'il vous plaît.	Your ticket, please.
J'ai perdu mon billet.	I've lost my ticket.
Vous n'avez pas composté vos billets.	You haven't date-stamped your tickets.

Note: For buying fuel, breakdowns and accidents see pages 78–79.

Une meilleure mémoire 6

Activité visuo-spatiale

Avant de faire cet exercice, révisez les pages 28 à 38.
Observez ce plan pendant une minute. Puis donnez-vous encore trois minutes pour écrire le nom des bâtiments qui vont dans ces cases:
1e 2b 3a 3f 4b 4c

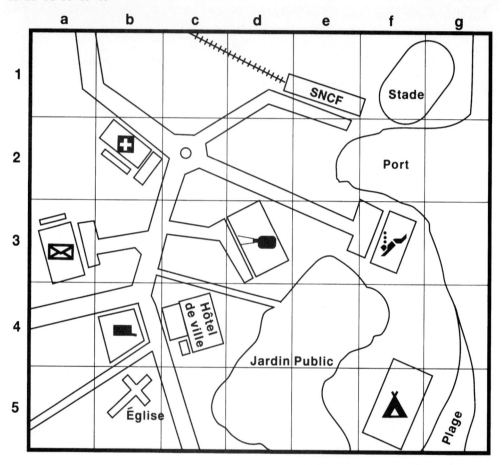

Solution à la page 90

THE WORLD OF WORK

◀ *Education and training* ▶

Future plans

le bac(calauréat)	French A-level equivalent		**compliqué**	complicated
un examen	exam		**donc**	so
un métier	job		**inutile**	useless
une profession	profession		**plus tard**	later
un résultat	result		**riche**	rich
le travail	work		**n'importe quoi**	anything
une université	university		**s'intéresser à**	to be interested in
			je voudrais	I'd like

Qu'est-ce que tu veux faire plus tard?	What do you want to do later?
Après les examens, j'espère rester au collège.	After the exams, I hope to stay at school.
L'année prochaine, j'espère commencer à préparer mon bac.	Next year, I hope to start to prepare for my A-levels.
Je vais faire anglais, français et histoire.	I'm going to do English, French and history.
Parce que je veux être professeur.	Because I want to be a teacher.

◀ *Careers and employment* ▶

Travelling to work

normalement	normally		**retourner**	to return
un problème	problem		**venir**	to come
quitter	to leave			

Comment venez-vous au collège?	How do you come to school?
D'habitude, je viens en vélo.	Usually, I come by bike.
Tu prends le bus pour aller au travail?	Do you take the bus to go to work?
Non, j'y vais à pied.	No, I walk there.
Normalement, ça prend trente minutes.	Normally, it takes 30 minutes.

Testez-vous

Ces personnes, que font-elles?

A) Elles regardent la télévision.
B) Elles achètent des billets.
C) Elles attendent dans le métro.
D) Elles compostent leurs billets.

Solution à la page 90.

Out of work

le chômage	unemployment	**un moment**	moment
un(e) chômeur(-euse)	someone who is unemployed	**chercher**	to look for
un emploi	job	**dur**	hard

Votre frère, que fait-il?	What does your brother do?
Il est au chômage.	He is unemployed.
Ça doit être très difficile.	That must be very difficult.
Oui, c'est dur.	Yes, it's hard.

Jobs and work experience

un bureau	office	**une usine**	factory
un camion	lorry	**la vie**	life
un(e) employé(-e)	employee	**dangereux(-se)**	dangerous
un(e) employeur(-euse)	employer	**faire**	to do
un métier	job	**faire un stage en entreprise**	to do work experience

Qu'est-ce qu'elle fait dans la vie?	What job does she do?
Elle travaille dans une usine.	She works in a factory.
Elle travaille quarante heures par semaine.	She works 40 hours per week.
Tu as déjà travaillé?	Have you already had a job?
J'ai travaillé dans un bureau pendant une semaine.	I've worked in an office for one week.
Je travaille le week-end dans une station-service.	At the weekend, I work in a petrol station.
J'y travaille depuis six mois.	I've been working there for six months.

Spare time jobs

un(e) caissier(-ère)	cashier	**bien payé**	well paid
faire du baby-sitting	to babysit	**mal payé**	badly paid
un journal	newspaper	**payer**	to pay
livrer	to deliver	**seulement**	only
un salaire	salary	**tout le monde**	everyone

Je ne travaille pas le week-end.	I don't work at the weekends.
Je livre des journaux tous les matins.	I deliver newspapers every morning.
J'ai souvent fait du baby-sitting.	I've often babysat.
On me paie trois livres par heure.	I get paid £3 per hour.
Je trouve que c'est intéressant mais assez dur.	I find it interesting but quite hard.

Future plans

la chance	luck		**ça dépend**	it depends
un(e) étudiant(-e)	student		**étudier**	to study
continuer	to continue		**passer**	to spend
décider	to decide			

Qu'est-ce que vous espérez faire après les examens?	What do you hope to do after the exams?
Je voudrais aller à l'université.	I'd like to go to university.
Je vais quitter le collège.	I'm going to leave school.
Si j'ai de bons résultats, j'irai au lycée.	If I get good results, I'll go to the 6th form college.
Qu'est-ce que tu espères faire?	What do you hope to do?

Jobs – yourself and your family

un agent de police	police officer		**une hôtesse de l'air**	air hostess
un avocat	lawyer		**un(e) infirmier(-ère)**	nurse
un(e) boucher(-ère)	butcher		**un(e) instituteur (-trice)**	primary school teacher
un(e) boulanger(-ère)	baker		**un(e) informaticien(-ne)**	computer operator
un chauffeur	driver		**un ingénieur**	engineer
un chef	cook, chef		**un(e) mécanicien(-ne)**	mechanic
un(e) coiffeur(-euse)	hairdresser		**un médecin**	doctor
une dactylo	typist		**un(e) ouvrier(-ère)**	worker
un(e) dentiste	dentist		**un(e) patron(-ne)**	boss
un(e) dessinateur (-trice)	designer		**un professeur**	teacher
un(e) électricien (-ne)	electrician		**un(e) secrétaire**	secretary
un(e) élève	pupil		**un(e) vendeur(-euse)**	salesman/woman, a shop assistant
un(e) épicier(-ère)	grocer		**un vétérinaire**	vet
un facteur	postman		**comme**	like; as
un(e) fermier(-ère)	farmer		**être**	to be
un(e) garagiste	garage worker or owner			
un garçon de café	waiter			

Mon père est infirmier.	My dad is a nurse.
Ma mère a toujours été informaticienne.	My mum has always been a computer operator.
Mon frère veut être mécanicien.	My brother wants to be a mechanic.
Ma belle-mère est vendeuse depuis trois ans.	My stepmother has been a shop assistant for three years.

Une meilleure mémoire 7

Activité logique

Avant de faire cet exercice, révisez les pages 40 à 42.
Regardez ces horloges. Il y a un ordre logique. Trouvez-le et écrivez l'heure.

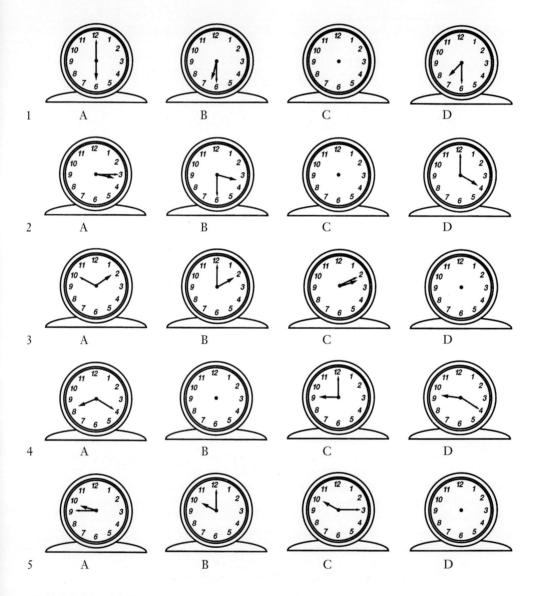

	A	B	C	D
1				
2				
3				
4				
5				

Solution à la page 90.

◄ *Advertising and publicity* ►

Advertisements

une affiche	poster		jeune	young
un dessin	drawing		magnifique	magnificent
une image	picture		meilleur	better; best
la publicité	publicity		pire	worse

À mon avis, cette publicité est formidable.	In my opinion, this publicity is great.
Je déteste cette photo.	I hate this photo.
Je n'aime pas l'image non plus.	I don't like the picture either.
La meilleure affiche est celle-ci.	The best poster is this one.

Publicity

une agence de voyages	travel agency		les renseignements (m)	information
une brochure	brochure		un touriste	tourist
un dépliant	leaflet		une visite	visit
une distraction	leisure activity		fermer	to close; to switch off
un jour férié	public holiday		ouvrir	to open; to switch on
une liste	list		se passer	to happen
un passeport	passport		nécessaire	necessary
une pièce d'identité	identity document		par personne	per person
un prix	price; prize			

Achetez aujourd'hui.	Buy today.
Renseignez-vous au syndicat d'initiative.	Get your information at the tourist information office.

◄ *Communication* ►

Telephone numbers

un indicatif	code		avoir	to have
un numéro	number		c'est le	it's
un téléphone	telephone		connaître	to know

Quel est votre numéro de téléphone?	What's your 'phone number?
C'est le dix, quatorze, trente, soixante-deux.	It's 10. 14. 30. 62.
Vous connaissez l'indicatif?	Do you know the code?

Answer a telephone call

allô	hello (on the telephone)		à l'appareil	speaking

Madame Collet à l'appareil.	Mrs Collet speaking.

Ask to speak to someone / Telephone messages

bonjour	hello		**laisser**	to leave
parler	to speak		**prendre**	to take
passer	to put someone through		**rappeler**	to call back
			occupé	engaged
avec	with		**qui**	who
là	there		**zéro**	zero; nought
un message	message		**le répondeur**	answer machine

Allô, je voudrais parler avec Jean, s'il vous plaît.	Hello, I'd like to speak with Jean, please.
Est-ce que je pourrais parler à Marie?	Could I speak to Marie?
Vous pourriez me passer Monsieur Lancien?	Could you put me through to Mr. Lancien?
Je vous le passe.	I'm putting you through.
C'est de la part de qui?	Who's speaking?
Voulez-vous laisser un message?	Would you like to leave a message?
Dites au directeur que Monsieur Gaillac a téléphoné.	Tell the manager that Mr. Gaillac called.
Demandez à Madame Berringer de me rappeler.	Ask Mrs. Berringer to call me back.
Vous pouvez me rappeler?	Can you call me back?

Une meilleure mémoire 8

Votre mémoire immédiate

Avant de faire cet exercice, révisez les pages 28 à 45.
Observez ces objets pendant deux minutes. Puis fermez le livre et essayez, en moins de quatre minutes, d'écrire une liste des objets. L'ordre n'est pas important.

Comparez votre liste avec les dessins.

Solution à la page 90.

THE INTERNATIONAL WORLD

◀ *Life in other countries and communities* ▶

Money and prices

un billet	note		**un franc**	franc
un bureau de change	exchange office		**la monnaie**	change
			une pièce	coin
un chèque de voyage	traveller's cheque		**des soldes**	sale
			mille	a thousand
un euro	euro			

Je voudrais changer vingt livres sterling.	I'd like to change £20.
Vous acceptez les chèques de voyage?	Do you accept traveller's cheques?
Avez-vous des pièces de cinq euros pour le téléphone?	Do you have any five euro coins for the telephone?

◀ *Tourism* ▶

Talk about holidays

le bord de la mer	seaside		**un séjour**	stay
un mois	month		**chez**	at the home of
la plage	beach		**voyager**	to travel
une promenade	walk; trip			

Vous avez passé de bonnes vacances?	Did you have a good holiday?
Je suis allé à l'étranger.	I've been abroad.
Où avez-vous été?	Where did you go?
Je suis allée en montagne avec mes parents.	I went to the mountains with my parents.
On a nagé dans le lac.	We swam in the lake.
Nous y avons passé quinze jours.	We spent two weeks there.
D'habitude, je vais au bord de la mer avec ma famille.	Usually I go to the seaside with my family.

Describe a previous holiday

en bateau	by boat		**dernier**	last
une caravane	caravan		**louer**	to rent; to hire
un gîte	holiday home		**rencontrer**	to meet
un souvenir	memory		**tous les jours**	every day

Où as-tu passé tes vacances l'année dernière?	Where did you spend your holidays last year?
Je suis allé en France avec ma famille.	I went to France with my family.
Nous avons loué un gîte.	We rented a holiday home.
Nous y avons passé une semaine.	We spent a week there.

Il a fait beau tous les jours.	The weather was good every day.
Nous avons vu des choses intéressantes.	We saw some interesting things.
C'était formidable.	It was great.

Excursions and places of interest

un monument	a monument		**voir**	to see
jamais	never		**plutôt**	rather
oublier	to forget		**pour moi**	for me

Vous avez fait des excursions?	Did you go on any excursions?
Oui, nous avons visité de beaux châteaux.	Yes, we visited some beautiful castles.
J'ai vu tous les monuments de Paris.	I saw all the monuments in Paris.
Pour moi, c'était plutôt ennuyeux.	For me, it was rather boring.

◀ *Accommodation* ▶

Are rooms available?

une chambre	room		**complet**	full
la place	room		**libre**	free
la clef	key			

Vous avez une chambre de libre, s'il vous plaît?	Do you have a room free, please?
Je m'excuse, mais c'est complet.	I'm sorry, but it's full.
Vous avez de la place pour deux personnes?	Do you have room for two people?

When and for how long

un jour	day		**du ... au**	from the ... to the
une nuit	night		**jusqu'à**	until
une semaine	week		**réserver**	to reserve
à partir de	from		**vouloir**	to want

Madame, Monsieur,
   Je voudrais réserver une chambre pour deux personnes dans votre hôtel, du vingt-huit avril au deux mai.
   Pourriez-vous confirmer cette réservation?
   Je vous prie d'agréer, Madame, Monsieur, l'expression de mes sentiments les meilleurs.

What sort of room

un balcon	balcony		**double**	double
une chambre	room		**pour une personne**	for one person
avec un grand lit	with a double bed		**pour deux personnes**	for two people

de famille	for a family
avec douche	with shower
avec salle de bains	with bathroom
la demi-pension	half board
une douche	shower

la pension complète	full board
un réveil	alarm clock
une vue	view
les W.C.	toilets

Avez-vous une chambre de famille?	Have you got a family room?
Nous voudrions une chambre avec salle de bains.	We'd like a room with a bathroom.
Si c'était possible, je voudrais une chambre avec vue sur la mer.	If it was possible, I'd like a room with a sea-view.

Ask the cost

le prix	price
coûter	to cost

compris	included
quel	what

Ça coûte combien par nuit?	How much does it cost per night?
Avec pension complète, c'est combien?	How much is it with full board?
Quel est le prix d'une chambre?	What is the price of a room?

Accept or reject a room

accepter	to accept
ça va	that's O.K.

prendre	to take
quelque chose de	something

Avez-vous quelque chose de moins cher?	Do you have anything cheaper?
D'accord, je la prends.	Agreed, I'll take it.

Identify yourself

britannique	British
une fiche	form
une fille	girl; daughter
un fils	son

au nom de	in the name of
un passeport	passport
remplir	to fill in
signer	to sign

J'ai réservé une chambre au nom de Jones.	I've reserved a room in the name of Jones.
Ça s'écrit J O N E S.	That is spelt J O N E S.
Nous sommes cinq: moi, ma femme, mon fils et nos deux filles.	There are five of us: me, my wife, my son and our two daughters.

Ask where facilities are

l'ascenseur	lift
le parking	car park
le restaurant	restaurant

les toilettes	toilets
se trouver	to be

Où se trouve le restaurant, s'il vous plaît?	Where is the restaurant, please?
Au rez-de-chaussée.	On the ground floor.
Il y a un parking à l'hôtel?	Is there a car park at the hotel?

Testez-vous

Vous arrivez à l' hôtel Métropol, à Calais.

Vous voulez pour et vous voulez savoir combien ça coûte. Que dites-vous?

Solution à la page 90.

Meal times			
de ..... à	from ..... to	**un repas**	a meal
le déjeuner	lunch	**la salle à manger**	dining room
le dîner	dinner	**servi**	served
le petit déjeuner	breakfast		

Le petit déjeuner est à quelle heure?	At what time is breakfast?
Le déjeuner est servi de midi à deux heures.	Lunch is served from midday until 2 o'clock.

Paying			
payer	to pay	**la note**	bill
pouvoir	to be able	**ne ... que**	only

Je peux avoir ma note, s'il vous plaît?	Please can I have my bill?
Ça fait combien?	How much does it come to?
Je n'ai que des chèques de voyage.	I only have traveller's cheques.

Book accommodation

les arrhes	deposit		**à la suite**	following
confirmer	to confirm		**tard**	late
d'avance	in advance		**tôt**	early
un fax	fax		**tout de suite**	at once

Est-ce que je pourrais réserver une chambre pour la nuit du premier août?	Could I reserve a room for the night of August 1st?
Je vous enverrai des arrhes tout de suite.	I'll send you a deposit straight away.
Pourriez-vous m'envoyer un fax pour confirmer la réservation?	Could you send me a fax to confirm the reservation?
Je vous prie d'agréer l'expression de mes sentiments les meilleurs	Yours faithfully

> Madame,
> À la suite de notre conversation au téléphone, je vous écris pour confirmer ma réservation d'une chambre double pour la nuit du trente juillet.
> Pourriez-vous m'envoyer la liste des prix et des renseignements sur l'hôtel?
> Je vous prie d'agréer, Madame, l'expression de mes sentiments les meilleurs.

Note: For youth hostels and campsites see page 88.

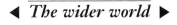

◀ *The wider world* ▶

Understand names of countries

For other countries, see page 9.

la Suisse	Switzerland		**le Canada**	Canada
l'Afrique (f)	Africa		**le Québec**	Quebec
l'Amérique (f)	America			

J'ai passé les vacances de Pâques en Suisse.	I spent the Easter holidays in Switzerland.
J'aimerais bien aller aux États-Unis.	I'd really like to go to the U.S.A.
Je n'ai jamais été au Canada.	I've never been to Canada.

Nationalities and languages

allemand	German		**français**	French
américain	American		**gallois**	Welsh
anglais	English		**grec(-cque)**	Greek
autrichien(-nne)	Austrian		**hollandais**	Dutch
belge	Belgian		**irlandais**	Irish
danois	Danish		**italien(-ienne)**	Italian
écossais	Scottish		**portugais**	Portuguese
espagnol	Spanish		**suédois**	Swedish
finlandais	Finnish		**suisse**	Swiss

Ma mère est française.	My mother is French.
J'ai un correspondant belge.	I've got a Belgian penfriend.
Je parle portugais.	I speak Portuguese.

◀ *Examination French* ▶

The list below contains the words which will be used in instructions and questions in your French exam. Make sure that you know them and this will make you faster and more successful!

Rubrics and Instructions

aider	to help	**trouver**	to find
aller	to go	**utiliser**	to use
choisir	to choose	**vérifier**	to check
cocher	to tick	**vouloir dire**	to mean
comparer	to compare		
compléter	to complete	**vous avez ...**	you have ...
conseiller	to advise	**vous avez reçu ...**	you have received ...
correspondre à	to correspond with	**vous entrez dans ...**	you go into ...
corriger	to correct	**vous êtes ...**	you are ...
décrire	to describe	**vous passez vos**	you are spending
demander à	to ask		your
dessiner	to draw	**vous voulez ...**	you want ...
devoir	to have to	**vous voulez**	you want to
dire	to say	**acheter ...**	buy ...
donner	to give	**anglais**	English
écouter	to listen	**français**	French
écrire	to write		
employer	to use	**un article**	article
entendre	to hear	**une carte**	map; card
être	to be	**une case**	box
expliquer	to explain	**une chose**	thing
faire	to do, to make	**un(e)**	penfriend
faire attention	to pay attention	**correspondant(e)**	
il s'agit de	it is about	**un crayon**	pencil
il y a	there is, there are	**le contraire**	opposite
imaginer	to imagine	**un dessin**	drawing
indiquer	to indicate	**un détail**	detail
inventer	to invent	**un dialogue**	dialogue
jouer	to play	**un dictionnaire**	dictionary
mettre dans le	to put into the	**un équivalent**	equivalent
bon ordre	correct order	**une erreur**	mistake
montrer	to show	**un exemple**	example
lire	to read	**un extrait**	extract
noter	to note	**une faute**	error
parler de ce que	to talk about what	**une flèche**	arrow
penser	to think	**une fois**	one time
pouvoir	to be able	**un Français**	French person
poser	to ask	**une grille**	grid
regarder	to look	**une question**	question
remercier	to thank	**une illustration**	illustration
remplir	to fill in	**une image**	picture
répondre	to answer	**une instruction**	instruction
savoir	to know (how to)	**une interview avec**	interview with
souligner	to underline	**une lettre**	letter
tourner	to turn	**un message**	message
traduire	to translate	**un mot**	word

une note	note; mark	ci-dessous	below
un numéro	number	ci-dessus	above
une page	page	combien?	how much? how many?
un panneau	notice; sign		
le passé	the past	comment	how
un peu	little	c'est	it is
une phrase	sentence	c'est quoi?	what is it?
un plan	plan	c'est-à-dire	that is to say
un point	point; full stop	à droite	on the right
une remarque	remark	d'abord	first of all
une réponse	answer	en bas	below
un rôle	role	en haut	above
une série	series	encore	again
le silence	silence	encore une fois	once more
le suivant	the next one	environ	about
un symbole	symbol	est-ce que?	is?
un thème	theme	à gauche	on the left
vacances à/en ...	holidays at/in ...	que	what, which
		quel	which, what
approprié	appropriate	qui	who, which
bien	well, good	quoi?	what?
bon(-nne)	good	Qu'est-ce que...?	What...?
correct	correct	Qu'est-ce que c'est?	What is it?
différent	different	leur	their; to them
exact	correct, exact	maintenant	now
faux(-sse)	false, wrong	ou	or
jeune	young	où	where
juste	just, correct	pas	not
mal	badly	plus	plus
négatif(-ive)	negative	pourquoi	why
précis	precise	puis	then
vrai	true	quand	when
		seulement	only
à	at, to, in	si	if
à quelle heure?	at what time?	sur	on
après	after	voici	here is, here are
autre chose	something else	vos	your
ce, cette, cet	this	votre	your
ces	these	vous	you
chaque	each	vraiment	really

Choisissez thème 1 ou thème 2.	Choose theme 1 or theme 2.
Cochez la phrase appropriée.	Tick the appropriate sentence.
Complétez les détails en français.	Complete the details in French.
Dans votre lettre vous devez ...	In your letter you must ...
Demandez les informations suivantes.	Ask for the following information.
Dessinez une flèche pour montrer quelle illustration va avec quel panneau.	Draw an arrow to show which illustration goes with which sign.
Écoutez l'exemple.	Listen to the example.
Écrivez l'équivalent en anglais.	Write the equivalent in English.
Écrivez environ ..... mots.	Write about ..... words.
Écrivez dans la case le numéro de l'illustration qui correspond à chaque instruction.	Write in the box the number of the picture which corresponds to each instruction.
Est-ce que les phrases sont vraies ou fausses?	Are the sentences true or false?
Lisez l'article.	Read the article.
Lisez les instructions.	Read the instructions.
Lisez les phrases suivantes.	Read the following sentences.
Répondez aux questions posées dans la lettre.	Answer the questions asked in the letter.
Répondez aux questions.	Answer the questions.
Si la remarque est fausse, écrivez une remarque correcte.	If the remark is wrong, write a correct remark.
Utilisez ces symboles pour faire un dialogue.	Use these symbols to make up a dialogue.
Vous allez entendre deux fois une série de petites conversations.	You are going to hear twice a series of short conversations.
Vous allez entendre deux jeunes Français qui parlent de leur	You are going to hear two young French people who are talking about their .....
Vous pouvez employer un dictionnaire si vous voulez.	You can use a dictionary if you wish.
Vous trouvez ces informations sur	You find this information about .....

EVERYDAY ACTIVITIES

◀ *Language of the classroom* ▶

Explain a word / Ask how it is pronounced

comment	how	**prononcer**	to pronounce
expliquer	to explain	**un truc**	thing
un machin	thing		

Vous pourriez m'expliquer ce mot?	Could you explain this word to me?
Qu'est-ce que cela veut dire?	What does that mean?
Ce machin-là, comment s'appelle-t-il?	What's that thing there called?
Cette phrase se dit comment, s'il vous plaît?	How is that sentence said, please?
Ça se prononce comment?	How is that pronounced?

Classroom activities

une case	box	**mettre dans le**	to put in the right
un dictionnaire	dictionary	**bon ordre**	order
une réponse	answer, reply	**poser**	to ask
un sondage	poll	**ramasser**	to collect
un tableau noir	blackboard	**à moi**	my turn
les travaux manuels	arts and crafts	**à toi**	your turn
cocher	to tick	**approprié**	appropriate
distribuer	to give out	**présent**	present

Qui commence?	Who starts?
C'est à moi.	It's my turn.
À toi, maintenant.	It's your turn now.
Tu travailles avec moi?	Will you work with me?
Je peux te poser une question?	Can I ask you a question?
J'ai fini.	I've finished.

◀ *School* ▶

Learning languages

se défendre	to get by	**le russe**	Russian
couramment	fluently	**le temps**	time
une langue	language		

Depuis combien de temps apprenez-vous le français?	For how long have you been learning French?

J'apprends le français depuis cinq ans.	I've been learning French for five years.
Vous connaissez d'autres langues étrangères?	Do you know any other foreign languages?
J'apprends l'allemand depuis presque trois ans.	I've been learning German for nearly three years.
J'aimerais bien apprendre le hollandais parce que ma grand-mère est hollandaise	I'd really like to learn Dutch because my grandmother is Dutch.
Je me défends en espagnol.	I get by in Spanish.
Je parle couramment l'italien.	I speak Italian fluently.

School timetables

avoir tort/raison	to be right/wrong		la rentrée	start of the school year
l'année scolaire	school year			
un trimestre	term		trop	too; too much; too many
obligatoire	compulsory			

Pour moi, le meilleur trimestre, c'est le deuxième.	For me, the best term is the second one.
À mon avis, il y a trop de matières.	In my opinion, there are too many subjects.
Moi, je pense que le français ne devrait pas être obligatoire.	I think that French should not be compulsory.
Qu'en pensez-vous?	What do you think about it?
Vous avez peut-être raison.	Perhaps you're right.

School subjects, rules and uniform

le droit	the right		porter	to wear
un lycée	6th form college		complètement	completely
une règle	rule		contre	against
un uniforme	uniform		pour	for
il vaut mieux	it is better to		ridicule	ridiculous

Êtes-vous pour ou contre l'uniforme obligatoire au collège?	Are you for or against compulsory uniform at school?
Je suis plutôt pour, parce que c'est plus facile et moins cher.	I'm rather in favour of it, because it's easier and cheaper.
Moi, je n'accepterai jamais l'uniforme.	I will never accept the uniform.
Je le trouve complètement ridicule.	I find it completely ridiculous.
Avoir des règles, c'est une bonne idée.	It's a good idea to have rules.
Mais il y a des règles bêtes.	But there are some stupid rules.
Par exemple, on devrait avoir le droit de porter ce qu'on veut.	For example, we should have the right to wear what we like.

Different types of school

un C.E.S	an 11–16 comprehensive school		mixte	mixed
			la plupart de	most
			polyvalent	comprehensive
l'éducation (f)	education		primaire	primary
l'enseignement (m)	teaching		privé	private
une maternelle	nursery school		relativement	relatively
la scolarisation	schooling		secondaire	secondary

Presque tous les jeunes français vont à la maternelle, à partir de trois ans.	Nearly all French children go to a nursery school, from the age of three.
Il y a relativement peu d'écoles privées, en France.	There are relatively few private schools in France.
La scolarisation est obligatoire de six à seize ans.	Schooling is compulsory from the age of 6 to 16.
La plupart des collèges sont mixtes et polyvalents.	Most secondary schools are mixed and comprehensive

◀ *Home life* ▶

Typical meals, meal times and eating habits

le cidre	cider		copieux (-ieuse)	copious
la mayonnaise	mayonnaise		préparer	to prepare
une sardine	sardine		sucré	sweet
une truite	trout		salé	salty

Chez nous, le petit déjeuner est un repas plutôt léger.	At our house, breakfast is a lightish meal.
D'habitude, le dîner est assez copieux.	Usually, dinner is quite substantial.
Normalement, je préfère les plats salés.	Normally, I prefer salted dishes.
Je n'aime pas manger trop tard.	I don't like to eat too late.

Helping around the house

aller chercher	to look for		la baignoire	bath
balayer	to brush		le chauffage central	central heating
donner un coup de main	to give a hand		une casserole	saucepan
			l'électricité (f)	electricity
essuyer	to wipe; to dry		un évier	sink
faire les courses	to do the shopping		le gaz	gas
faire la lessive	to do the washing		le ménage	housework
repasser	to iron		une poêle	pan
utiliser	to use		la vaisselle	washing up

Je peux vous donner un coup de main?	Can I give you a hand?
Tu sais repasser?	Can you iron?
Non, mais je pourrais faire les lits.	No, but I could make the beds.
Vous pourriez m'aider?	Could you help me?
Tu pourrais nettoyer les poêles?	Could you clean the pans?
J'irai faire les courses, si tu veux.	I'll go and do the shopping if you like.
Mets la vaisselle dans l'évier, s'il te plaît.	Put the washing-up in the sink, please.

How members of the family help at home

faire du bricolage	to do it yourself	**un coup de main**	hand; help
faire la cuisine	to cook	**la pelouse**	lawn
mettre la table	to set the table	**juste**	fair
tondre	to mow	**tout**	everything

Chez nous, c'est ma mère qui fait la plupart du travail.	At our house, it's my mother who does most of the work.
C'est toujours mon père qui fait du bricolage.	It's always my dad who does the odd jobs.
D'habitude, mon frère lave et moi j'essuie.	Usually, my brother washes and I dry.
Tu trouves que c'est juste, ça?	Do you think that that is fair?

Say if you share a room

la chance	luck	**seul**	alone
partager	to share		

Je partage une chambre avec ma soeur.	I share a room with my sister.
J'ai une chambre pour moi tout seul.	I have a room just for me.
Tu as de la chance!	You're lucky!
J'aimerais bien avoir une chambre pour moi toute seule.	I'd really like to have a room just for me.

Describing daily routine

se brosser les dents	to brush one's teeth	**se laver**	to wash
se coucher	to go to bed	**se lever**	to get up
s'habiller	to get dressed	**se réveiller**	to wake up

Normalement, je me couche vers onze heures.	Normally I go to bed at about 11 o'clock.
Dimanche dernier, je me suis levé à cinq heures du matin pour aller à la pêche.	Last Sunday I got up at 5 a.m. to go fishing.
Demain je vais me lever à sept heures.	Tomorrow I'm going to get up at seven o'clock.

◀ *Media* ▶

Narrate a theme or plot of a book

au début	at the start	**il s'agissait de**	it was about
à la fin	at the end	**s'approcher de**	to approach
un auteur	author	**commencer par**	to begin by
le héros	hero	**tout à coup**	suddenly
la héroïne	heroine	**tuer**	to kill
une histoire	story	**principal**	main; principal
un personnage	character	**récemment**	recently
un(e) policier(-ière)	policeman(-woman)		

J'ai lu récemment un très bon roman.	I've recently read a very good novel.
De quoi s'agissait-il?	What was it about?
Il avait lieu aux États-Unis.	It was set in the U.S.A.
Au début de l'histoire une femme a appris	At the start of the story, a woman learned
au téléphone qu'on cherchait à la tuer.	on the 'phone that someone was trying to kill her.
Le héros, c'était le policier qui l'a sauvée.	The hero was the policeman who saved her.

Testez-vous

Vous lisez cette rubrique dans un magazine. Expliquez le titre 'Miss 100 000 volts' à un ami qui ne parle pas français.

Solution à la page 90.

Narrate a simple item of news

arriver	to happen
battre	to beat
il paraît que	it seems that
il y a eu	there has been, there was
une grève	a strike
la guerre	war
parmi	amongst
un télé-journal	a TV news programme
d'après	according to

Tu as entendu ce qui est arrivé hier?	Have you heard what happened yesterday?
Il paraît qu'il y aura bientôt de nouveaux jeux-vidéo.	It seems that there will soon be some new video games.
D'après le journal, il y a eu un accident terrible.	According to the newspaper, there has been a terrible accident.
On a dit qu'il y avait des grèves partout.	They said that there were strikes everywhere.

LIV RES

Miss 100 000 volts

C'est ainsi qu'ils nomment la chaise électrique aux États-Unis. Ils, ce sont les gardiens et condamnés qui plaisantent sur cette machine qui veille au bout du couloir. Il suffit de suivre la ligne verte au sol pour se rendre au dernier rendez-vous.
Stephen King, spécialiste des atmosphères lourdes, a décidé de s'essayer au feuilleton. "La Ligne verte" devrait vous laisser en haleine plusieurs mois. L'auteur affirme ne pas connaître encore la conclusion de son histoire.

A. O.-G.

"La ligne verte", premier épisode, Stephen King, éditions Librio, 10 F.

Newspapers, magazines, books, TV programmes, radio, music and performers

avoir horreur de	to hate	un feuilleton	serial
dernier	last; latest		

Tu as entendu le dernier disque de ...?	Have you heard the latest record by ...?
Tu as vu l'émission à la télé, hier soir?	Did you see the programme on TV last night?
Qu'est-ce que tu en as pensé?	What did you think of it?
Moi, je l'ai trouvée plutôt ennuyeuse.	Well, I found it rather boring.
J'ai horreur de ce groupe.	I hate that group.
Je ne lis jamais les journaux.	I never read the newspapers.

Narrate the main features of a TV or radio programme

un chantier	site	**le RMI**	unemployment pay
un documentaire	documentary	**la terre**	the earth
un coup	trick; blow	**émouvant**	moving
la durée	length	**exclu**	excluded
un espoir	hope	**véritable**	real, true
une fouille	dig; search	**confier**	to confide, to trust
une mutation	change	**plonger**	to plunge, to dive
un paysan	small farmer;		
	agricultural worker		

Testez-vous

Lisez ces extraits. Ensuite, sans consulter un dictionnaire, répondez aux questions suivantes.

1 À quelle heure commence le documentaire sur un projet pour aider des gens qui n'ont pas de travail?
2 D'où est venue l'inspiration du film qui est annoncé?
3 Quel est le titre de l'émission qui a eu lieu aux États-Unis il y a plus de cinquante ans?

Solution à la page 90.

Clés de l'actualité, No. 159, juin 1995
Télé 7 jours, 1 er au 7 juillet, 1995

La guerre des boutons ■■

C'est la rentrée des classes et, comme chaque année, deux écoles se livrent une guerre où tous les coups sont permis. Pour ce "remake" américain du film d'Yves Robert, l'action est transposée en Irlande. Une bonne idée que l'on doit au producteur David Puttnam. A l'origine de cette exploration du monde de l'enfance, le roman de Louis Pergaud, "La guerre des boutons" (éd. Mercure de France).

20.30 HISTOIRE **La Terre**

1939 : les vaches maigres...
De 1939 à 1942, Robert Flaherty filma l'Amérique agricole. Cette période de mutations techniques transforma la paysannerie traditionnelle, plongée dans une crise profonde, en une véritable industrie de la terre.   4576043

21.10 Jules César au secours des chômeurs Pendant quelques mois, six chômeurs de longue durée sont sortis du cercle infernal du RMI pour travailler sur un chantier de fouilles archéologiques. Une rencontre émouvante avec ces exclus du système économique qui ont confié à la caméra leurs difficultés, leurs espoirs et leurs visions du monde...
21.40 J'avais dix amis
23.00 Les Ailes de légende Boeing 707
23.55 Voleurs d'organes
  0.55 Mémoires d'images, images d'un roi (1)

◀ *Health and fitness* ▶

Arrange to consult a doctor, dentist or chemist

un cabinet de	surgery	**la santé**	health
consultation		**consulter**	to consult
une clinique	clinic	**se sentir**	to feel
une consultation	consultation	**urgent**	urgent
un(e) pharmacien(ne)	chemist		

Je me sens vraiment malade.	I feel really ill.
Je pense que je devrais aller voir un médecin.	I think I ought to go and see a doctor.
Je pourrais venir voir le dentiste, s'il vous plaît?	Could I come and see the dentist, please?

Il n'est pas libre aujourd'hui.	He isn't free today.
C'est urgent.	It's urgent.
Il faut que je le voie aujourd'hui.	I must see him today.
Vous pourriez venir à dix-sept heures trente?	Could you come at 5.30 p.m?

At a doctor's, dentist's or chemist's

la bouche	mouth	**une piqûre**	injection; sting
une blessure	injury	**un sirop**	syrup
le corps	body	**le sparadrap**	sticking plaster
un coup de soleil	sunburn	**un tube**	tube
la diarrhée	diarrhoea	**se blesser**	to hurt oneself
une épaule	shoulder	**se brûler**	to burn oneself
la fièvre	temperature	**se casser**	to break
la grippe	influenza, 'flu	**conseiller**	to advise
une insolation	sunstroke	**couper**	to cut
le mal de mer	seasickness	**se fouler**	to twist
le visage	face	**mourir**	to die
la voix	voice	**se noyer**	to drown
une aspirine	aspirin	**se passer**	to happen
un cachet	pill	**pleurer**	to cry, to weep
un comprimé	tablet	**se reposer**	to rest
le coton hydrophile	cotton wool	**souffrir**	to suffer
une crème	cream	**vomir**	to be sick
une cuillerée	spoonful	**docteur**	what you say to a doctor
un médicament	medicine		
une opération	operation	**médecin**	doctor
une ordonnance	prescription	**grave**	serious
un pansement	dressing	**mort**	dead
une pastille	pastille	**normal**	normal

Qu'est-ce qui s'est passé?	What has happened?
Je me suis cassé le bras.	I've broken my arm.
J'ai passé trop de temps au soleil.	I spent too much time in the sun.
Vous avez de la fièvre?	Have you got a temperature?
Vous avez la grippe.	You have 'flu.
Je vous conseille d'aller au lit et de vous reposer.	I advise you to go to bed and rest.
Je vous donnerai une ordonnance.	I'll give you a prescription.

Healthy and unhealthy lifestyles

une calorie	calorie	**en forme**	in good shape
un régime	diet	**maigre**	thin
le sommeil	sleep	**régulier**	regular
une vitamine	vitamin	**courir**	to run
l'alcool	alcohol		

une drogue	drug	s'entraîner	to train
le tabac	tobacco	éviter	to avoid
le tabagisme	nicotine addiction	pratiquer un sport	to practise a sport
absolument	absolutely	suivre	to follow
équilibré	balanced	ni ... ni	neither ... nor

Il faut absolument éviter le tabac et l'alcool.	It's absolutely essential to avoid tobacco and alcohol.
C'est une bonne idée de pratiquer régulièrement un sport.	It's a good idea to practise a sport regularly.
Moi, je n'ai jamais pris et je ne prendrai jamais de drogues.	I've never taken and will never take any drugs.
Il vaut mieux suivre un régime équilibré.	It's best to follow a balanced diet.
J'essaie d'être ni trop maigre ni trop gros.	I try to be neither too thin nor too fat.
Que fais-tu pour rester en forme?	What do you do to stay in good shape?

◀ *Food* ▶

React to offers of food or drink, giving reasons

l'agneau	lamb	le goût	taste, flavour
une amande	almond	une odeur	smell
une cuisse de grenouille	frog's leg	le parfum	taste
		allergique	allergic
un escargot	snail	appétissant	appetising
une moule	mussel	saignant	rare (of meat)
un oignon	onion	volontiers	with pleasure
une truite	trout	ça m'est égal	I don't mind
une carafe	carafe	ça suffit	that's enough

Encore quelques oignons?	A few more onions?
Non, merci, ça suffit.	No thanks, that's enough.
Je suis allergique aux moules.	I'm allergic to mussels.
Je n'ai jamais goûté la truite aux amandes.	I've never tasted trout with almonds.
Mais je voudrais bien l'essayer.	But I'd really like to try it.
Je prends des médicaments et l'alcool m'est interdit.	I'm taking some medicines and am not allowed alcohol.

Appreciation and compliments

mes compliments	my compliments	inoubliable	unforgettable
félicitations	congratulations	le chef	chef, cook
féliciter	to congratulate	surtout	above all

C'était vraiment délicieux.	It was really delicious.
J'ai surtout aimé le dessert.	I especially liked the dessert.
Merci beaucoup pour un repas inoubliable.	Many thanks for an unforgettable meal.

Ask for more or say that you have had enough

reprendre	to take some more	il reste	there is left

Est-ce qu'il reste de l'agneau?	Is there any lamb left?
J'en reprendrais un peu avec plaisir.	I'd have a little more of it with pleasure.
J'adore les frites, je peux en prendre beaucoup?	I love the chips, can I have a lot of them?
J'ai déjà trop (assez) mangé.	I've already eaten too much (enough).
Ça va comme ça, merci.	That's fine as it is, thanks.

Ask for a table / State preference for seating

une personne	person	l'extérieur	the outside
réserver	to reserve	l'intérieur	the inside
Vous êtes combien?	How many of you are there?	une section non-fumeur	a non-smoking area
Nous sommes cinq.	There are five of us.	une terrasse	a terrace
dehors	outside		

Vous avez une table pour une personne?	Do you have a table for one?
Je voudrais réserver une table pour quatre personnes.	I'd like to reserve a table for four people.
Auriez-vous une table sur la terrasse?	Would you have a table on the terrace?
Je préférerais une table à l'intérieur.	I'd prefer a table inside.
Nous voudrions être dans une section non-fumeur.	We'd like to be in a non-smoking area.

Complain, giving reasons

le directeur	manager	lent	slow
la directrice	manageress	satisfait	satisfied
le patron	owner	se mettre en colère	to get angry
(la patronne)		se plaindre	to complain
entièrement	entirely	protester	to protest
inadmissible	unacceptable		

Nous n'avons pas commandé de cidre.	We didn't order any cider.
Je voudrais voir le directeur.	I'd like to see the manager.
Je voudrais me plaindre.	I'd like to complain.
J'ai commandé un steak saignant et on m'a apporté un steak bien cuit.	I ordered a rare steak and they brought me a well-done steak.
Le service était très lent.	The service was very slow.
Je ne suis pas du tout satisfait.	I'm not at all satisfied.
Le dessert était affreux.	The dessert was awful.
On nous a mis dans une section fumeur.	We were put in a smoking section.

Ask about service charges

un couvert	cover charge	un pourboire	tip

La boisson est comprise?	Is the drink included?
Le prix du couvert n'est pas inclus.	The price of the cover charge is not included.

PERSONAL AND SOCIAL LIFE

◀ *Self, family and friends* ▶

State, and understand others stating gender and marital status

âgé	aged	demi-soeur	half sister
aîné	elder	une épouse	wife
cadet(-te)	younger	un époux	husband
célibataire	single; unmarried	une femme	woman; wife
divorcé	divorced	un neveu	nephew
féminin	feminine	une nièce	niece
fiancé	engaged	la naissance	birth
marié	married	un petit-fils	grandson
masculin	masculine	une petite-fille	grandaughter
séparé	separated	le sexe	sex
une dame	lady	un veuf	widower
demi-frère	half brother	une veuve	widow

Ma soeur aînée a deux enfants, un garçon de trois ans et une fille de huit mois.	My elder sister has two children, a boy of three and a daughter of eight months.
Mon frère est célibataire.	My brother is not married.
Mes parents sont divorcés depuis deux ans.	My parents have been divorced for two years.
Ma grand-mère est veuve.	My grandmother is a widow.

Spell out names, streets and towns

épeler	to spell	le domicile	home address
un boulevard	boulevard		

Voici mon adresse: le trente et un, rue Colbert.	Here's my address: 31, rue Colbert.
Comment s'écrit le nom de la rue?	How do you spell the name of the street?
J'habite un petit village qui s'appelle Cauterets.	I live in a small village called Cauterets.
Tu pourrais épeler le nom du village?	Could you spell the name of the village?

Describe character and personality

le caractère	character	nerveux(-euse)	nervous; nervy
actif(-ve)	active	optimiste	optimistic
curieux(-euse)	curious; nosey	paresseux(-euse)	lazy; idle
désagréable	disagreeable	pessimiste	pessimistic
doux(-ce)	soft; gentle	sage	good; well behaved
étrange	strange	sûr	reliable; trustworthy
fier(fière)	proud	compter	to count
fou (folle)	mad	embêter	to annoy
furieux(-euse)	furious	si	so
honnête	honest	tellement	so

Comment as-tu trouvé l'amie de Pierre?	How did you find Pierre's girl friend?
Je l'ai trouvée plutôt nerveuse.	I found her rather nervous.
Martine est très sûre, on peut compter sur elle.	Martine is very reliable, you can count on her.
Marc m'embête, il est toujours si sage.	Marc gets on my nerves, he's always so good.

Express feelings about others

s'entendre	to get on together		responsable	responsible
inquiéter	to worry		surprenant	surprising
respecter	to respect		un sourire	smile
sembler	to seem		un(e) voisin(e)	neighbour
paraître	to appear		chacun	each one
bizarre	strange		naturellement	naturally
élégant	elegant		parfaitement	perfectly
inquiet(-ète)	worried		pire	worse; worst
malheureux (-euse)	unhappy		prêt	ready
mécontent	unhappy		réussir	to succeed
pauvre	poor			

Tu t'entends bien avec tes parents?	Do you get on well with your parents?
Je m'entends mal avec ma belle-mère.	I get on badly with my stepmother.
Que pensez-vous de mon beau-père?	What do you think of my stepfather?
Il me paraît parfaitement bien.	He seems perfectly fine to me.
Je suis sûr qu'il va réussir.	I'm sure he will succeed.

Testez-vous

Sur ce panneau, il y a des lettres qui manquent. Pouvez-vous compléter ces mots?

1. PARC NA_IONAL   3. PÊ_HE   5. CHEV_L
2. MONTA_NE   4. CAMPI_G

Solution à la page 90.

◀ *Free time, holidays and special occasions* ▶

Hobbies, interests and leisure activities

un ballon	ball		un western	western
une bande dessinée (B.D.)	comic strip		une collection	collection
un(e) champion(-ne)	champion		un instrument de musique	musical instrument
le cricket	cricket		se baigner	to swim
un(e) cycliste	cyclist		jouer aux échecs	to play chess
un(e) joueur(-euse)	player		se promener	to go for a walk
un film d'espionnage	spy film		ne ... que	only
un opéra	opera			

J'aime surtout me promener à la campagne.	Above all, I like walking in the country.
À mon avis, le meilleur sport du monde, c'est le cricket.	In my opinion, the best sport in the world is cricket.
Mon père ne regarde que des westerns.	My dad only watches westerns.
J'aime tout, sauf le hockey.	I like everything except hockey.

Clubs

une activité	activity		une maison de jeunes	youth club
le ballet	ballet		un orchestre	orchestra
le billard anglais	snooker		une réunion	meeting
les boules	French bowls		une société	society
le chœur	choir		apprécier	to appreciate
une conférence	lecture		avoir le temps de	to have time to
une cotisation	club subscription		fréquenter	to frequent, to go out with
la jeunesse	youth; young people		participer à	to take part in

Vous êtes membre d'un club?	Are you a member of a club?
Oui, le week-end je participe à des réunions d'une société musicale.	Yes, at weekends I take part in meetings of a musical society.
La semaine dernière j'ai entendu une conférence excellente sur le jazz moderne.	Last week I heard an excellent lecture on modern jazz.
Je vais toutes les semaines à un club de jeunes.	I go every week to a youth club.

Holidays and activities

un congé	holiday		le tourisme	tourism
un guide	guide		s'en aller	to go away
un jardin zoologique	zoo		se faire bronzer	to get a suntan
le monde	world		se souvenir	to remember
une pellicule	film (for a camera)		car	as; because
la planche à voile	windsurfing		chaque	each; every
un son et lumière	'son et lumière' (sound and light show)			

Je sors peu, car je n'ai pas le temps avec tous mes devoirs.	I don't go out much as I don't have the time with all my homework.
L'été dernier, je suis allé en Espagne et je me suis fait bronzer.	Last summer I went to Spain and got a suntan.
L'année prochaine, nous ferons du tourisme dans l'ouest de la France.	Next year, we'll go touring in the west of France.
Quand j'aurai un jour de congé, j'irai voir le son et lumière.	I'll go and see the son et lumière (sound and light) show when I have a day's holiday.

Sporting events

assister à	to attend; to go to	un spectateur	spectator
s'ennuyer	to be bored	le stade municipal	town stadium
frapper	to hit	ensemble	together
jeter	to throw	insupportable	unbearable
la mi-temps	half time	tant mieux	so much the better
une randonnée	walk	tant pis	too bad
sauter	to jump	un arbitre	referee

Samedi dernier, j'ai assisté à un match de hockey.	Last Saturday, I went to see a hockey match.
Je me suis ennuyé.	I was bored.
Tant pis!	That's too bad!
Si tu n'aimes pas les randonnées, il vaut mieux rester à la maison.	If you don't like walks, it's better to stay at home.
À mon avis, le jeu était insupportable.	In my opinion, the game was unbearable.

Information about excursions and visits

une agence de voyages	travel agency	une vallée	valley
un S.I. (syndicat d'initiative)	tourist information office	ça m'est égal	I don't mind
		n'importe quand	any time
		médiéval	medieval

Avez-vous des dépliants sur les excursions dans la vallée de la Loire?	Do you have any leaflets about excursions to the Loire valley?
Quand voudriez-vous partir?	When would you like to leave?
N'importe quand.	At any time.
Vous pourriez aller voir le château médiéval.	You could go and see the medieval castle.
Le prix des repas est compris?	Is the cost of meals included?

Discuss preferences and alternatives for going out

une petite annonce	small ad	exagérer	to exaggerate
une pièce de théâtre	play	n'importe où	anywhere
un sous-titre	sub-title	suggérer	to suggest
un titre	title		

Il y a un bon film en ville, on y va ensemble?		There's a good film in town, shall we go to it together?	
C'est en version originale, avec des sous-titres en français.		It's with the original soundtrack and French sub-titles.	
J'aimerais mieux aller voir une pièce de théâtre.		I'd rather go and see a play.	
Si on restait à la maison voir ce documentaire à la télé?		How about staying at home and watching this documentary on TV?	

Money

fauché	broke, hard up	emprunter	to borrow
une augmentation	increase; rise	puisque	since
un budget	budget	vendre	to sell

Je ne pourrai pas sortir ce soir puisque je suis fauchée.	I won't be able to go out this evening as I'm broke.
Il ne me reste que deux francs.	I've only got two francs left.
Je pourrais peut-être emprunter de l'argent à mon frère.	Perhaps I could borrow some money from my brother.
Il faut que je demande une augmentation.	I must ask for an increase.
Je n'ai jamais assez d'argent.	I've never got enough money.

◄ *Personal relationships and social activities* ►

Ask permission to do things

conduire	to drive	je t'en prie; je vous en prie	not at all; of course
avoir envie de	to want to		
célébrer	to celebrate	sers-toi; servez-vous	help yourself
enregistrer	to record		
faire de l'auto-stop	to hitch-hike	défendu de	forbidden to
interdire	to forbid	le maquillage	make-up
jeter	to throw	la permission	permission
permettre	to allow	une vidéo	video
stationner	to park		

Est-ce que je pourrais utiliser le magnétoscope pour enregistrer une émission?	Could I use the video to record a programme?
Puis-je mettre du maquillage?	Can I wear make-up?
Vous permettez?	Is it all right?
On peut fumer ici?	Can one smoke here?
Non, c'est défendu.	No, it's forbidden.
Puis-je sortir?	May I go out?

Apologise

assurer	to assure	**se mettre en colère**	to get angry
déranger	to disturb; to inconvenience	**pardonner**	to forgive
		exprès	on purpose
s'excuser	to apologise	**mon Dieu!**	my God!
s'inquiéter	to worry	**oh, là, là!**	oh dear!

Excusez-moi, je n'aurais pas dû me mettre en colère.	Forgive me, I shouldn't have lost my temper.
Je m'excuse, c'était de ma faute.	I'm sorry, it was my fault.
Pardon, madame, je ne faisais pas attention.	Sorry, madam, I wasn't paying attention.
Je vous assure que je ne l'ai pas fait exprès.	I assure you that I didn't do it on purpose.

Discuss your problems

un adolescent	adolescent	**étonner**	to astonish
une allocation familiale	family allowance	**gêner**	to embarrass; to bother
une bande	gang	**insulter**	to insult
la carrière	career	**mentir**	to tell lies
une catastrophe	catastrophe	**respecter**	to respect
la confiance	confidence	**supporter**	to bear, to stand
le courrier du coeur	agony column	**vivre**	to live
une crise	crisis	**déçu**	disappointed
les gens	people	**dégoûtant**	disgusting
le loyer	rent	**économique**	economic
la politique	politics	**étonnant**	amazing
une solution	solution	**eux/elles**	them
approuver	to approve of	**évident**	obvious
en avoir marre de	to be fed up with	**fâché**	angry, annoyed
critiquer	to criticise	**grâce à**	thanks to
créer	to create	**malgré**	in spite of
croire	to believe	**même**	even; same
se débrouiller	to get by	**politique**	political
discuter	to discuss	**social**	social
se disputer	to quarrel, to argue		

J'en ai marre des gens qui font la guerre.	I'm sick of people who make war.
Je trouve que c'est dégoûtant.	I find that it is disgusting.
Je me dispute souvent avec mes parents.	I often quarrel with my parents.
Ma mère se plaint toujours de moi.	My mother is always complaining about me.
Qu'est-ce que tu me conseilles de faire?	What do you advise me to do?

◀ *Arranging a meeting or activity* ▶

Entertainment options

avoir envie de	to feel like	**le judo**	judo
un bal	dance; a ball		

On peut faire du judo ici?	Can you do judo here?
J'ai envie d'aller à une disco: c'est possible?	I feel like going to a disco: is that possible?
On pourrait écouter de la musique, si tu préfères.	We could listen to music if you prefer.

Negotiate a meeting

prendre rendez-vous	to arrange to meet	**de nouveau**	again
de bonne heure	early	**ravi**	delighted
certainement	certainly	**dépendre**	to depend
sans doute	without doubt	**empêcher**	to prevent
sur le point de	about to; on the point of	**une intention**	intention

Je suis sur le point d'aller en ville: tu veux m'accompagner?	I'm just about to go into town: do you want to come with me?
On peut prendre rendez-vous pour ce soir?	Can we arrange to meet this evening?
D'accord, mais il faut que je rentre de bonne heure.	O.K., but I must be home early.
Si on se rencontrait demain matin?	How about seeing each other tomorrow morning?

◀ *Leisure and entertainment* ▶

Find out what is on

une comédie	comedy	**le Minitel**	Minitel (computer-based database available on telephone and computer)
le guide des spectacles	the guide to what's on		

Qu'est-ce qu'on peut faire, samedi soir?	What can we do on Saturday evening?
Il y a un bon concert en ville, le week-end prochain?	Is there a good concert in town next weekend?
Si on achetait le guide des spectacles?	How about buying the guide to what's on?
Nous pourrions consulter le Minitel.	We could consult the Minitel.

Starting and finishing times

une pièce	play		**une séance**	performance

La pièce commence à quelle heure?	What time does the play begin?
La séance finit à quelle heure?	What time does the performance end?

Opinions

plaire	to please		**le rôle**	role; part
un comédien	actor		**un succès**	success
un choix	choice		**franchement**	frankly
un entracte	interval		**à cause de**	because of
laid	ugly		**ce n'est pas la peine**	it's not worth it
un musicien	musician			

Comment as-tu trouvé le concert?	What did you think of the concert?
Le film t'a plu?	Did you like the film?
Ce que j'ai aimé surtout c'était l'histoire.	What I liked above all was the story.
Tu as fait un très bon choix.	You made a very good choice.
Celui qui a joué le rôle du héros était sensass.	The one who played the part of the hero was fantastic.
Malgré les mauvais comédiens, la pièce était bien.	In spite of the bad actors, the play was good.

Narrate the main features of a film or play

autrefois	in the past		**une rubrique**	column in a magazine or newspaper
l'avenir (m)	the future			
le lendemain	the following day			
le passé	the past		**lutter**	to fight, to struggle
un siècle	century		**se marier avec**	to marry
un accident	accident		**oser**	to dare
l'amour (m)	love		**venir de**	to have just
une armée	army		**dès que**	as soon as
un risque	risk		**finalement**	finally

C'est un film qui a lieu dans l'avenir, au trentième siècle.	It's a film which takes place in the future, in the 30th century.
Le lendemain, le héros a lutté contre l'armée.	The next day, the hero fought the army.
Heureusement, il n'y a pas eu d'autres accidents.	Fortunately, there were no more accidents.
Elle a réussi parce qu'elle a osé prendre des risques.	She succeeded because she dared to take some risks.
Finalement, ils se sont mariés.	In the end, they got married.

THE WORLD AROUND US

◀ *Home town, local environment and customs* ▶

Understand a description of a town or region

un aéroport	airport	un site	site; beauty spot
une ambiance	atmosphere	une station	resort
un attrait	attraction	bruyant	noisy
une capitale	capital	énorme	enormous
un champ	field	estival	summer
une colline	hill	hivernal	winter
un fleuve	major river	national	national
le fond	back; bottom	profond	deep
une forêt	forest	régional	regional
une frontière	frontier; border	tranquille	quiet
une horloge	clock	construire	to build
une île	island	manquer	to miss; to lack
un palais	palace	offrir	to offer
une reine	queen	le long de	alongside
un roi	king		

Your country and others

l'agriculture (f)	agriculture	ensoleillé	sunny
une bibliothèque	library	humide	damp
un chemin de fer	railway	pittoresque	picturesque
un commerçant	shopkeeper	sec (sèche)	dry
un détail	detail	autour de	around
un ferry	ferry	au milieu de	in the middle of
la fumée	smoke	partout	everywhere
une industrie	industry	à peine	hardly
le paysage	countryside	pire	worse; worst
la qualité	quality	décrire	to describe
un sommet	summit	remarquer	to notice
commercial	commercial		

Pourriez-vous décrire la ville que vous avez visitée?
Could you describe the town which you visited?

À Colognac, l'agriculture est importante.
In Colognac agriculture is important.

Ici, en hiver, le climat est sec et ensoleillé.
Here, in winter, the climate is dry and sunny.

Le paysage autour du village est très beau.
The countryside around the town is very pretty.

Where you live

propre	clean		**autrement dit**	in other words
sale	dirty		**cependant**	however
un changement	change		**croire**	to believe
la côte	coast		**avoir honte**	to be ashamed

Que penses-tu de la ville où tu vis?	What do you think about the town where you live?
Je crois que c'est absolument magnifique parce qu'il y a plein de choses à faire.	I think it's absolutely magnificent because there's lots to do.
Moi, j'ai honte de vivre ici parce que c'est sale et mort.	I'm ashamed to live here because it's dirty and dead.
Il n'y a rien à faire pour les jeunes.	There's nothing for young people to do.

Important festivals

le réveillon du nouvel an	New Year's eve		**juif (juive)**	Jewish
la veille de Noël	Christmas eve		**musulman**	Muslim
catholique	catholic		**protestant**	protestant
chrétien (-ienne)	Christian		**la synagogue**	synagogue
			se déguiser	to dress up

Nous allons à la messe.	We go to mass.
Nous mangeons un repas spécial.	We eat a special meal.
On se déguise.	We dress up in fancy dress.

Weather forecasts

une amélioration	improvement		**frais (fraîche)**	cool
une averse	downpour		**lourd**	heavy
une brume	mist		**neigeux(-euse)**	snowy
la chaleur	heat		**nuageux(-euse)**	cloudy
un changement	change		**orageux(-euse)**	stormy
le ciel	sky		**pluvieux(-euse)**	rainy
une éclaircie	sunny spell		**variable**	variable
la moitié	half		**ailleurs**	elsewhere
un orage	storm		**au-dessous de**	below
la précipitation	precipitation; rain		**au-dessus de**	above
une prévision	forecast		**maximum**	maximum
un risque	risk		**minimum**	minimum
une tempête	storm		**supérieur**	above; higher than
le tonnerre	thunder		**devenir**	to become
la visibilité	visibility		**prévoir**	to predict
clair	clear		**retourner**	to return
couvert	covered; cloudy			

On prévoit quel temps pour demain?	What weather is forecast for tomorrow?
Il paraît qu'il pleuvra.	It seems that it will rain.
On dit qu'il y aura des orages et des éclaircies.	They say that there will be storms and sunny spells.
Après-demain, il fera beau et ensoleillé.	The day after tomorrow, it will be fine and sunny.
Dans la moitié sud du pays, le ciel sera couvert.	In the southern half of the country, the sky will be cloudy.

◀ *Finding the way* ▶

How to get to a specific place

un coiffeur	hairdresser	un passant	passer by
un consulat	consulate	un trottoir	pavement
un kiosque	kiosk	se perdre	to get lost
une laverie	launderette	reconnaître	to recognise
automatique		sens unique	one way
un opticien	optician		

Où se trouve exactement le consulat britannique?
Where exactly is the British consulate?

Vous suivez le chemin de fer et vous tournez à droite à la clinique.
You follow the railway line and you turn right at the clinic.

Il vaut mieux demander au syndicat d'initiative.
It's best to ask at the tourist information office.

◀ *Shopping* ▶

Find particular goods and departments within a store

un ascenseur	lift	un gant de toilette	face flannel
un escalier roulant	escalator	un jouet	toy
un(e) client(e)	customer	un micro-ordinateur	microcomputer
un rayon	department in a store	le papier à lettres	letter paper
les soldes	sales	une pile	battery
une vitrine	shop window	une plante	plant
une crémerie	dairy	le shampooing	shampoo
un déodorant	deodorant	un tricot	jumper; sweater
un gant	glove	libre service	self service

Où est le rayon maquillage, s'il vous plaît?
Where is the make-up department, please?

Où puis-je acheter du papier à lettres?
Where can I buy some letter paper?

Au sous-sol.
In the basement.

Vous pourriez me faire un paquet cadeau?
Could you gift-wrap it for me?

Discuss shopping habits and preferences

aimer mieux	to like better; to prefer	un avantage	advantage
		un inconvénient	disadvantage
faire du	to go window	un panneau	sign; notice
lèche-vitrines	shopping		

Le samedi après-midi, je fais souvent du lèche-vitrines.
On Saturday afternoon, I often go window shopping.

À mon avis, le meilleur magasin pour les vêtements, c'est ... .
In my opinion, the best shop for clothes is ... .

À ... les vendeurs sont plus gentils.
At ... the shop assistants are nicer.

Le supermarché ... reste ouvert jusqu'à vingt-deux heures.
The ... supermarket stays open until 10 pm.

L'inconvénient, c'est que cette boutique n'ouvre pas le dimanche.
The disadvantage is that that shop does not open on Sundays.

Buy or leave something

un blouson	bomber jacket; blouson	**un porte-monnaie**	purse
une botte	boot	**un sac à main**	handbag
une ceinture	belt	**bon marché**	cheap
un costume	suit	**parfait**	perfect
un portefeuille	wallet	**en soie**	made of silk

Ce sac à main est parfait, je le prends.	This handbag is perfect, I'll take it.
Je ne le prendrai pas, merci, c'est trop cher pour moi.	I won't take it, thank you, it's too expensive for me.
J'aime bien cette ceinture mais elle n'est pas assez longue.	I quite like this belt, but it's not long enough.
Auriez-vous quelque chose de meilleur marché?	Would you have anything cheaper?
Je l'aimerais mieux s'il était en cuir.	I'd like it better if it were made of leather.

Return unsatisfactory goods, giving reasons and asking for a refund or replacement

en bon état	in good condition	**échanger**	to exchange
une garantie	guarantee	**garantir**	to guarantee
une réclamation	complaint	**rembourser**	to reimburse
un reçu	receipt	**remplacer**	to replace
un trou	hole	**abîmé**	damaged; spoiled
casser	to break	**déchiré**	torn

Je voudrais me plaindre.	I'd like to complain.
J'ai acheté ce blouson ici hier.	I bought this bomber jacket here yesterday.
Pourriez-vous me le remplacer?	Could you replace it for me?
Regardez, c'est déchiré.	Look, it's torn.
Quand je l'ai acheté, je n'ai pas vu ce trou.	When I bought it, I didn't see this hole.
J'aimerais mieux être remboursé.	I'd prefer to get my money back.
Oui, j'ai gardé le reçu, le voici.	Yes, I've kept the receipt, here it is.

Testez-vous

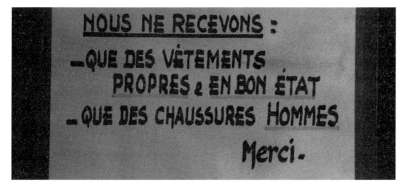

Vous voyez ce panneau dans la vitrine d'un magasin. Traduisez-le en anglais pour un ami qui ne le comprend pas. Ensuite devinez quelle sorte de magasin c'est.

Solution à la page 90.

Discounts, special offers, reductions and sales

une offre spéciale	special offer		**les soldes (f)**	sales
un prix pilote	special, experimental price		**gratuit**	free
une remise	discount		**moins 10%**	less 10%

Aujourd'hui nous offrons une remise de dix pour cent sur tous les articles au rayon vêtements.

Today we are offering a discount of 10% on everything in the clothing department.

Soldes du nouvel an.

New Year sales.

◀ *Public services* ▶

Sending letters, postcards and parcels

mettre à la poste	to post		**un formulaire**	form
un colis	parcel		**l'Australie**	Australia

Ça coûterait combien d'envoyer ce colis en Australie?

How much would it cost to send this parcel to Australia?

J'ai déjà rempli la fiche, la voilà.

I've already filled in the form, here it is.

Vous voulez l'envoyer par avion?

Would you like to send it airmail?

Exchange money or travellers' cheques

un billet de banque	banknote		**un guichet**	counter
une carte bancaire	bank card		**la monnaie**	change
une carte de crédit	credit card		**une pièce d'identité**	identity document
un dollar	dollar		**vaut**	is worth

Combien vaut la livre sterling aujourd'hui?

How much is the pound sterling worth today?

Je voudrais changer cent dollars américains.

I'd like to change 100 American dollars.

C'est quel guichet pour changer des chèques de voyage?

Which counter is it to change traveller's cheques.

Vous avez une pièce d'identité?

Do you have an identification document?

Voici mon passeport.

Here's my passport.

Ask for specific coins

un billet de cent francs	100 franc note		**une pièce de cinquante centimes**	50 centime coin

Pourriez-vous me donner des pièces de cinq francs?

Could you give me some five franc coins?

J'aimerais mieux avoir des billets de cent francs.

I'd prefer some 100 franc notes.

Report a loss or theft

un appareil photo	camera	un bureau des objets trouvés	lost property office
une bague	ring	la forme	shape
une bracelet	bracelet; strap	la marque	make
une caméra vidéo	video camera	une récompense	reward
un carnet de chèques	cheque book	un vol	theft
une clé (une clef)	key	carré	square
un flash	flash for a camera	en métal	made of metal
une montre	watch	(tout) neuf	(brand) new
une poche	pocket	rectangulaire	rectangular
un sac à dos	rucksack	marquer	to mark
une valise	case	voler	to steal
		ceci	this
		dedans	inside

J'ai perdu ma caméra vidéo.	I've lost my video camera.
On m'a volé ma valise.	Someone has stolen my case.
Je l'ai perdu avant-hier.	I lost it the day before yesterday.
Je l'ai laissé dans le bus.	I left it in the bus.
Elle est toute neuve et le bracelet est en métal.	It's brand new and the strap is made of metal.
Pourriez-vous décrire votre sac à dos?	Could you describe your rucksack?
Il est assez grand et bleu clair.	It's quite big and light blue.
Qu'est-ce qu'il y avait dedans?	What was inside it?
Il y avait un carnet de chèques et des clés.	There was a cheque book and some keys.
L'appareil est de quelle marque?	What make is the camera?
C'est un Kodak.	It's a Kodak.
Je l'ai cherché partout.	I've looked everywhere for it.

Getting things cleaned and repaired

une assurance	insurance	une laverie automatique	launderette
une cordonnerie	cobbler's	un pressing	dry cleaner
faire réparer	to get repaired	un reçu	receipt
faire nettoyer	to get cleaned		

Vous pouvez me nettoyer ce pantalon?	Can you clean these trousers for me?
Il sera prêt quand?	When will it be ready?
Où est-ce que je peux faire réparer mon rasoir électrique?	Where can I get my electric razor repaired?
J'ai besoin d'un reçu pour l'assurance.	I need a receipt for the insurance.

◀ *Getting around* ▶

Information about public transport

un compartiment	compartment		**un tarif**	price; tariff
une couchette	couchette in a train		**une voiture**	car (in a train)
un omnibus	slow, stopping train		**un wagon-lit**	sleeping car
un porteur	porter		**un wagon-restaurant**	dining car
une portière	door		**à l'heure**	on time
un TGV	fast train		**manquer**	to miss
un supplément	supplement		**en provenance de**	coming from

J'ai manqué mon train.	I've missed my train.
Le prochain train pour Le Havre part à quelle heure?	What time does the next train for Le Havre leave?
Il faut payer un supplément?	Do you have to pay a supplement?
On peut manger dans ce train-là?	Can you eat in that train?
Je voudrais réserver une couchette.	I'd like to reserve a couchette.
C'est un wagon non-fumeur?	Is it a no-smoking carriage?
Attention! Le train en provenance de Lille arrivera en gare, voie numéro sept, avec neuf minutes de retard.	Attention, please! The train from Lille will arrive at platform seven, with a delay of nine minutes.

Travel by public transport

un aéroport	airport		**un hovercraft**	hovercraft
un bateau	boat		**un pilote**	pilot
une déviation	diversion		**le port**	port; harbour
la douane	customs		**un vol**	flight
un douanier	cutoms officer		**en classe touriste**	in tourist class
une hôtesse de l'air	air hostess		**voler**	to fly

Le prochain ferry pour l'Angleterre part à quelle heure?	When does the next ferry for England leave?
Je voudrais réserver une place pour une voiture et trois personnes.	I'd like to reserve a place for a car and three people.
Je voudrais acheter un billet pour le prochain vol pour Londres.	I'd like to buy a ticket for the next flight to London.
Classe touriste, s'il vous plaît.	Tourist class, please.

Common forms of transport

un moyen de transport	means of transport		**écologique**	ecological
avoir mal au coeur	to be sick		**polluer**	to pollute
avoir le mal de mer	to be seasick		**rendre**	to make; to return
			pratique	handy; practical

Moi, je n'aime pas prendre le bateau parce que je souffre du mal de mer.	I don't like taking a boat because I suffer from seasickness.
Le train est plus écologique que l'autobus.	The train is more ecological than the bus.
Les bus polluent terriblement l'atmosphère.	Buses badly pollute the atmosphere.
Le métro est plus rapide et moins cher que le bus.	The underground is faster and cheaper than the bus.

At a service station

faire le plein	to fill up	**un lavage automatique**	automatic wash
le deux-temps	two-stroke fuel for motorbikes	**une moto**	motorbike
l'essence (f)	petrol	**un pneu**	tyre
le gas-oil	diesel	**une pompe**	pump
l'ordinaire (m)	ordinary petrol	**un(e) pompiste**	attendant in service station
le sans plomb	lead-free petrol	**la pression**	pressure
une station-service	service station	**un scooter**	scooter
le super	top grade petrol	**une autoroute**	motorway
l'air (m)	air	**une carte routière**	road map
une batterie	car battery	**une déviation**	deviation; diversion
un coffre	car boot	**conduire**	to drive
l'huile (f)	oil	**vérifier**	to check

Faites le plein de sans plomb.	Fill it up with lead-free.
Cent francs d'ordinaire.	100 francs worth of premium.
Quarante litres de super.	40 litres of top grade petrol.
Pompe numéro neuf, je vous dois combien?	Pump number nine, how much do I owe you?
Voulez-vous vérifier l'eau et la pression des pneus?	Would you check the water and the tyre pressures?
Pour aller d'ici à l'autoroute, s'il vous plaît?	How do I get from here to the motorway, please?

A breakdown

en panne	broken down	**un frein**	brake
en panne d'essence	out of petrol	**un moteur**	motor; engine
une route	road	**une roue**	wheel
un camion	lorry	**un pare-brise**	windscreen
un mécanicien	mechanic	**une roue de secours**	spare wheel
une route nationale	main road; A-road	**freiner**	to brake
quelque chose	something	**marcher**	to work
une crevaison	puncture	**crevé**	punctured
un essuie-glace	windscreen wiper		

Ma voiture est tombée en panne.	My car has broken down.
Qu'est-ce qu'il y a?	What's wrong?
Le moteur fait un bruit bizarre.	The engine is making a strange noise.
Il y a quelque chose qui ne marche pas.	Something isn't working.
Les freins ne marchent pas.	The brakes aren't working.
Nous sommes sur la route nationale sept, à quinze kilomètres à l'ouest de Fréjus.	We're on A-road number seven, 15 kilometres west of Fréjus.
C'est une Ford blanche.	It's a white Ford.
Vous pouvez envoyer quelqu'un?	Can you send someone?

Testez-vous

Cette jeune fille, où travaille-t-elle?

Solution à la page 90.

	Report an accident		
une ambulance	ambulance	**la priorité à droite**	priority to the right
un(e) blessé(e)	injured person	**un témoin**	witness
une collision	collision	**des travaux**	roadworks
un conducteur	driver	**au feu!**	fire!
un moto-cycliste	motorcyclist	**assuré**	insured
un piéton	pedestrian	**blessé**	injured
un véhicule	vehicle	**gravement**	seriously
un virage	bend	**soudain**	suddenly
l'assurance (f)	insurance	**circuler**	to drive
un constat	accident report form	**glisser**	to slip; to skid
la fin	end	**avoir peur**	to be afraid, frightened
les gendarmes (m)	police		
un permis de conduire	driving licence	**heurter**	to bump into; to hit
		ralentir	to slow down
la police-secours	emergency services	**rouler**	to drive
les pompiers	fire brigade	**stationner**	to park

Il y a eu un accident.	There has been an accident
C'est sur l'autoroute huit à dix kilomètres à l'est de Nice.	It's on motorway eight, ten kilometres east of Nice.
Un camion a heurté une voiture.	A lorry has hit a car.
La voiture était arrêtée au bord de la route.	The car was stopped at the side of the road.
Le camion roulait très vite.	The lorry was driving very fast.
Le conducteur a ralenti mais il n'a pas pu s'arrêter à temps.	The driver slowed down but he couldn't stop in time.
La visibilité était mauvaise à cause du brouillard.	Visibility was bad because of the fog.
Il faut appeler police-secours.	We must call for the emergency services.

THE WORLD OF WORK

◀ *Further education and training* ▶

Information about further education and training

un BTS	advanced vocational certificate, taken after two years of higher education	**les études (f)**	studies
		une filière	path
		une grande école	specialist higher education college
un chiffre	number	**un ingénieur**	engineer
une classe préparatoire	class to prepare for entry exams to higher education	**un IUT**	technical college
		une licence	degree
		encadrer	to supervise; to frame
une école normale	teacher training college	**quelqu'un**	someone
		supérieur	higher
l'état (m)	the state	**universitaire**	university; academic

Discuss education and training

un brevet	certificate; diploma	**un diplôme**	diploma
un certificat	certificate	**une faculté (de médecine)**	(medical) faculty
la classe terminale	6th form		
des cours commerciaux	commercial, business studies	**se plaire**	to be happy
		en sixième	in Year 7

Tu t'es plu au collège?	Have you been happy at school?
Oui, la plupart du temps, c'était bien.	Yes, most of the time it was fine.
Quand j'étais en troisième, j'aimais tout.	When I was in Year 10, I liked everything.
J'ai surtout aimé les sciences.	I've especially liked the sciences.
Que pensez-vous faire l'année prochaine?	What are you thinking of doing next year?
J'espère aller en classe terminale et préparer mon bac.	I hope to go to the 6th form college and prepare for my A-levels.
Si je réussis aux examens, j'irai à l'école normale.	If I succeed in my exams, I'll go to teachers' training college.
Qu'est-ce que vous espérez étudier à l'université?	What do you hope to study at university?
Je ne sais pas encore: la médecine ou la chimie, peut-être.	I don't know yet: medicine or chemistry, perhaps.

Testez-vous

Lisez cet extrait. Dites ensuite quel chiffre complète chaque phrase.

Par exemple: 1 – C

1 Un étudiant d'université coûte … francs par an.
2 Un étudiant dans une école technique coûte … francs par an.
3 Un étudiant qui espère être ingénieur coûte … francs par an.
4 Quelqu'un dans une classe préparatoire pour une grande école coûte … francs par an.

A) Soixante-seize mille trois cents.
B) Cinquante-deux mille cinq cents.
C) Trente et un mille.
D) Soixante-dix mille six cents.

Solution à la page 90.

CHIFFRES

31 000 francs

C'est le prix que coûte un étudiant d'université au budget de l'État chaque année. D'autres filières, davantage encadrées, reviennent plus cher : 52 500 F pour un étudiant d'IUT, 56 000 F pour celui de BTS, 70 600 F pour celui des classes préparatoires aux grandes écoles et 76 300 francs pour les ingénieurs des filières universitaires.

Les clés de l'actualité, no. 172, 1995.

◀ *Careers and employment* ▶

Explain choice of study or training

un doute	doubt		**faible**	weak
une note	mark		**fort**	good at; strong
les progrès (m)	progress		**prouver**	to prove
capable	capable			

Qu'est-ce que tu vas faire, l'année prochaine?	What are you going to do next year?
Tu vas étudier quelles matières?	Which subjects are you going to study?
Si tout va bien aux examens, je ferai sans doute histoire, espagnol et sciences économiques.	If all goes well at the exams, I'll no doubt do history, Spanish and economics.
J'ai toujours de bonnes notes en maths.	I always have good marks at maths.

Express hopes and plans for the future

gagner ma vie	to earn my living		**un laboratoire (de langues)**	(language) laboratory
une façon	way			

Qu'est-ce que vous espérez faire plus tard?	What do you hope to do later?
Je ne vois pas mon avenir d'une façon très claire.	I don't see my future in any very clear way.
Dans les mois qui viennent je vais travailler dur pour les examens.	In the coming months I'm going to work hard for the exams.

Après les études obligatoires, j'aimerais bien aller à l'université.	At the end of my compulsory schooling, I'd like to go to university.
Je voudrais gagner ma vie.	I'd like to earn my living.
J'espère travailler dans une banque.	I hope to work in a bank.

Jobs and work experience

un atelier	workshop		fatigant	tiring
une entrevue	interview		un stage en entreprise	work experience
la formation	training			
un poste	job; post		à temps partiel	part-time

Pourquoi travaillez-vous, le week-end?	Why do you work at the weekend?
Je travaille parce que j'aime avoir de l'argent à dépenser.	I work because I like to have money to spend.
J'ai déjà travaillé dans un café.	I've already worked in a café.
Normalement, je travaille environ dix heures par semaine.	Normally, I work for about ten hours per week.
Le travail est intéressant mais fatigant.	The work is interesting but tiring.
Je cherche un poste à temps partiel.	I'm looking for a part-time job.

Opinions about different jobs

les affaires	business		un(e) employé(e)	employee
une ambition	ambition		une ferme	farm
un coiffeur	hairdresser (male)		la sécurité	security
une coiffeuse	hairdresser (female)		un syndicat	a trade union
le commerce	commerce		devenir	to become
un décorateur	decorator			

Être dactylo, c'est un très bon métier.	Being a typist is a very good job.
La vie d'un ouvrier est dure.	A workman's life is hard.
Il paraît que les coiffeurs sont bien payés.	It appears that hairdressers are well paid.
Pour moi, la sécurité est essentielle.	For me, security is essential.
Ce que je cherche, c'est une bonne carrière.	What I'm looking for is a good career.

Enquire about the availability of suitable work

un salaire	salary		temporaire	temporary
une situation	situation		vacant	vacant
permanent	permanent			

Je cherche un emploi permanent dans un bureau.	I'm looking for a permanent job in an office.
Auriez-vous un poste vacant?	Would you have a vacancy?
Je ferais n'importe quoi.	I'd do anything.
Je serai libre à partir du premier août.	I'll be free from the 1st of August.
Pourriez-vous me donner des détails sur le salaire?	Could you give me some details about the salary?
J'ai déjà travaillé dans un grand magasin en Angleterre.	I've already worked in a department store in England.
Je cherche quelque chose de temporaire.	I'm looking for something temporary.

Occupations

un agriculteur	agricultural worker	**un militaire**	soldier
un(e) marchand de fruits	fruit seller	**une ouvreuse**	cinema usherette
		un sapeur-pompier	fire fighter

Qu'est-ce que ta mère fait dans la vie?	What does your mother do for a living?
Elle travaille dans une bibliothèque.	She works in a library.
Mon beau-père est militaire: il est dans l'armée de l'air.	My step-father is a soldier: he's in the air force.
Mon frère était dans le commerce.	My brother was in commerce.

Advantages and disadvantages

un avantage	advantage	**à mi-temps**	half-time
un inconvénient	disadvantage	**à plein temps**	full-time
sûr	secure		

Les infirmières doivent souvent travailler la nuit.	Nurses often have to work at night.
L'enseignement est assez sûr et bien payé.	Teaching is quite secure and well paid.
La journée d'un agriculteur peut être très longue.	A farm worker's day can be very long.
L'avantage c'est que les médecins sont bien payés.	The advantage is that doctors are well paid.
Si je travaillais dans une usine je ne serais pas heureux.	If I worked in a factory, I wouldn't be happy.

◀ *Advertising and publicity* ▶

Advertisements

un comptable	accountant	**une pub**	advertisement; TV commercial
un c-v	c.v. (curriculum-vitae)	**un spot télévisé**	TV commercial
exiger	to require, demand	**tenir**	to keep
rechercher	to seek	**la vente**	sale; selling

◀ *Communication* ▶

Using the phone, fax or E-mail

la tonalité	dialling tone	**un annuaire**	telephone directory
appeler	to call	**un coup de téléphone**	phone call
composer le numéro	to dial the number		
décrocher le combiné	to pick up the receiver	**le courrier électronique**	E-mail
raccrocher	to replace the receiver	**un fax**	fax
		un modem	modem

un ordinateur	computer
une seconde	second
une télécopie	fax

un télécopieur	fax machine
contacter	to contact
ne quittez pas	hold on

Vous pouvez toujours me contacter par téléphone.	You can always contact me by telephone.
Envoyez-moi un message par courrier électronique.	Send me a message by E-mail.
Quel est votre numéro de fax?	What's your fax number?
Vous trouverez notre numéro dans l'annuaire.	You'll find our number in the directory.
Appelez-moi demain matin si vous êtes libre.	Call me tomorrow morning if you're free.

Obtain coins or a phone-card

une cabine téléphonique	'phone booth
une pièce de un franc	1 franc coin

une télécarte	phone-card
une unité	unit

Est-ce que vous auriez des pièces de dix francs pour le téléphone?	Would you have some ten franc coins for the phone?
Une télécarte, s'il vous plaît.	A phone-card, please.
À combien d'unités?	For how many units?
À cinquante unités, si vous en avez.	For 50 units, if you have any.

Testez-vous

Vous voyez ceci dans une cabine téléphonique qui se trouve devant une poste. Où pouvez-vous acheter une télécarte sans problème?

Solution à la page 90.

THE INTERNATIONAL WORLD

◀ *Life in other countries and communities* ▶

Typical foods

la charcuterie	pork meats		un pique-nique	picnic
la farine	flour		une recette	recipe
un four	oven		le vin rosé	rosé wine
un four à micro-ondes	microwave oven		doux (douce)	mild
			piquant	spicy
un ingrédient	ingredient		varié	varied
un melon	melon		faire cuire	to cook
la merguez	North African spiced sausage		mélanger	to mix
			servir	to serve
la pâtisserie	pastry			

Un plat typique chez nous, c'est le Yorkshire pudding.	A typical dish in our country is Yorkshire pudding.
C'est une sorte de crêpe.	It's a sort of pancake.
On le mange avec du boeuf ou comme dessert, avec de la confiture.	It's eaten with beef or as a dessert, with jam.
On le fait avec de la farine, du lait, des oeufs et du sel.	You make it with flour, milk, eggs and salt.
On mélange les ingrédients avec une fourchette.	You mix the ingredients with a fork.
Et on le fait cuire dans un four très chaud.	And you cook it in a very hot oven.

Important social conventions

santé	good health		un chrysanthème	chrysanthemum
à la tienne	to your good health		une nappe	table cloth
à la vôtre	to your good health		couper	to cut
un appétit	appetite		garder	to keep
une convention	convention		offrir	to offer; to give

Quand on mange, en France, y a-t-il des conventions spéciales?	When eating in France, are there any special conventions?
En France, on ne devrait pas couper la salade ou le pain.	In France, you should not cut salad or bread.
Pendant un repas, on devrait garder les mains sur la table quand on ne mange pas.	During a meal, you should keep your hands on the table when you're not eating.
On met le pain sur la table ou sur la nappe, il n'y a pas d'assiette spéciale.	We put bread on the table or on the table cloth, there isn't a special plate.
Normalement, on offre des fleurs à son hôtesse, mais jamais de chrysanthèmes.	Normally, one gives flowers to one's hostess, but never chrysanthemums.

◀ *Tourism* ▶

Information about excursions

un tour	tour	**s'informer**	to get information
faire une promenade	to go for a trip	**guidé**	guided

Nous voudrions visiter la Dordogne.	We'd like to visit the Dordogne region.
Il y a une excursion guidée qui part après-demain.	There's a guided excursion which leaves the day after tomorrow.
Le prix des hôtels et des repas est compris?	Is the price of hotels and meals included?
D'où partira l'autocar?	Where will the coach leave from?

Request tourist publicity

un camping	campsite	**un site**	beauty spot; a site of historical or archaeological interest
une carte	map		
une étoile	one star	**avoir l'intention**	to intend

Madame, Monsieur,

J'ai l'intention de venir passer quelques jours dans votre région, avec ma famille, au mois de juillet prochain.

Pourriez-vous m'envoyer des renseignements sur les campings dans la région et des dépliants sur les sites à visiter et les excursions à faire?

En vous remerciant d'avance, je vous prie d'agréer, Madame, Monsieur, l'expression de mes sentiments les meilleurs.

Avez-vous une carte de la région?	Do you have a map of the region?
Qu'est-ce qu'il y a à voir, dans la région?	What is there to see in the region?
Vous avez des dépliants sur la ville?	Do you have any leaflets about the town?

Opinions about excursions and places of interest

une destination	destination	**un tableau**	painting
un endroit	place	**autour de**	around
l'intérêt (m)	interest	**préféré**	favourite

Qu'est-ce qu'il y a à voir dans la région?	What is there to see in the region?
Ma destination préférée, c'est le château de	My favourite destination is.... castle.
Il y a une bonne collection de tableaux du dix-neuvième siècle.	There's a good collection of 19th century paintings.
Et le paysage autour est très pittoresque.	And the countryside around is very picturesque.
Moi, je trouve que le musée national de chemin de fer est intéressant.	I think that the national railway museum is interesting.

Testez-vous

Pour vous distraire

Aujourd'hui	Demain	Tous les jours
▷ **ROQUEFORT-LES-PINS**	▷ **BAR-SUR-LOUP**	▷ **MONACO**
Jardin des Décades. — A 21 h, l'amicale des sapeurs pompiers organise son grand bal annuel. Entrée gratuite. L'après-midi, concours de boules.	**Place du village.** — Le 15, bal gratuit, à 21 h avec orchestre Rockline.	**Jardin Exotique.** — Ouvert tous les jours de 9 heures à 19 heures (grottes, musée d'anthropologie préhistorique).

NICE-MATIN, samedi 14 août 1993

Vous êtes en vacances, à Nice, et vous voyez cette rubrique dans le journal. Lisez-la et répondez aux questions suivantes.
1 Que pourriez-vous faire ce soir, à partir de neuf heures, si vous alliez à Roquefort-les-Pins?
2 Que pourriez-vous faire tous les jours, à Monaco?
3 Où pourriez-vous aller danser sans payer?

Solution à la page 90.

Discuss a holiday: past or future

à l'étranger	abroad	**beaucoup de monde**	a lot of people
un insecte	insect	**déçu**	disappointed
une mouche	fly	**fou (folle)**	mad
la poussière	dust	**revenir**	to return
un(e) propriétaire	owner		

Nous sommes allés en Afrique du Nord.	We went to North Africa.
C'était une catastrophe à cause de la chaleur et des insectes.	It was a disaster because of the heat and the insects.
Le premier jour, nous nous sommes baignés.	The first day, we swam.
Le lendemain, nous avons fait une promenade en car.	The next day, we went on a coach trip.
Nous étions assez déçus.	We were quite disappointed.
Et l'année prochaine, où irez-vous?	And where will you go next year?
Nous irons sans doute à l'étranger.	We'll no doubt go abroad.

Express preferences for different holidays

actif (-ive)	active	**de grand luxe**	very luxurious
en avoir marre	to be sick of	**meublé**	furnished
un choix	a choice	**il vaut mieux**	it's better

Moi, je préfère les vacances à l'étranger.	I prefer foreign holidays.
À mon avis, il vaut mieux rester en Grande-Bretagne.	In my opinion, it's better to say in Britain.
J'adore aller dans un hôtel de grand luxe.	I love going to a very luxurious hotel.
J'aimerais mieux louer un appartement meublé.	I'd rather rent a furnished flat.
J'ai horreur des vacances actives.	I hate active holidays.
Si j'avais le choix, j'irais toujours en Espagne.	If I had the choice, I'd always go to Spain.
J'en ai marre de rester à la maison.	I'm sick of staying at home.

◀ *Accommodation* ▶

Arrange accommodation at hotels, youth hostels and campsites

une auberge de jeunesse	youth hostel		**un emplacement**	site; location; plot
un dortoir	dormitory		**le Michelin rouge**	hotel guide
un drap	sheet		**une prise de courant**	electric plug
un sac de couchage	sleeping bag		**une tente**	tent
par jour	per day		**aménagé**	fully equipped
par personne	per person		**camper**	to camp
une caravane	caravan		**municipal**	municipal

Avez-vous de la place pour deux adultes et un enfant?	Do you have room for two adults and one child?
Je regrette, mais c'est complet.	I'm sorry, but it's full.
Il nous faut un grand emplacement pour notre tente.	We need a big site for our tent.
Vous pouvez louer des draps et un sac de couchage.	You can hire some sheets and a sleeping bag.
C'est combien par personne et par jour?	How much is it per person per day?
Il y a encore de la place au camping municipal.	There is still room at the municipal campsite.

Rules and regulations

un bac à vaisselle	washing-up sink		**un règlement**	rule
un bloc sanitaire	toilet block		**une sortie de secours**	emergency exit
un(e) gardien(-ienne)	warden		**s'adresser à**	to contact
un lavabo	wash basin		**déranger**	to disturb; to inconvenience
une salle de jeux	games room			
une cuisinière à gaz	gas cooker		**à emporter**	to take away
un incendie	fire		**fumer**	to smoke
un matelas pneumatique	inflatable mattress		**en cas de**	in case of
un rasoir électrique	electric razor		**potable**	drinking; drinkable

En cas d'incendie, sortez tout de suite par la sortie de secours la plus proche. Ne prenez pas l'ascenseur.	In the event of fire, go out at once through the nearest emergency exit. Do not take the lift.
Il faut quitter la chambre avant midi le jour du départ.	You have to leave the room before midday on the day you leave.
Tout le monde doit aider à faire le ménage.	Everyone must help to do the housework.
Pas de bruit après vingt-deux heures.	No noise after 10 p.m.
Il est interdit de fumer dans les dortoirs.	Smoking is forbidden in the dormitories.
En cas de problème, s'adresser au gardien.	In the case of any problems, contact the warden.
Laissez les lavabos propres.	Leave the wash basins clean.

◀ *The wider world* ▶

Environmental issues

une enquête	survey		une bombe	bomb
l'environnement	environment		une centrale	power station
une planète	planet		un essai	test
la protection	protection		un exposé	presentation
une baleine	whale		intéressé par	interested in
un dauphin	dolphin		nucléaire	nuclear
un éléphant	elephant		passionné par	really concerned about
un lion	lion		faire peur	to frighten
un panda	panda		protéger	to protect
un tigre	tiger		recycler	to recycle
un zoo	zoo		la circulation	traffic
en danger	in danger; endangered		un embouteillage	traffic jam
la nature	nature		la pollution	pollution
un océan	ocean			

Je suis passionnée par les animaux en danger. I'm really concerned about endangered animals.
Les centrales nucléaires me font peur. Nuclear power stations frighten me.
Qu'en penses-tu? What do you think about them?
Je suis d'accord avec toi. I agree with you.

Understand global issues

l'aide (f)	aid; help		la paix	peace
le crime	crime		un premier ministre	prime minister
une crise	crisis		un président	president
le dégât	damage		le racisme	racism
une drogue	drug		un(e) réfugié(-e)	refugee
l'économie	the economy		la religion	religion
une élection	election		le sida	Aids
le gaz d'échappement	exhaust fumes		la tolérance	tolerance
la fumée	smoke		la violence	violence
le charbon	coal		concerné par	concerned about
un niveau	level		international	international
l'ONU	UNO		quant à	as for
une organisation	organisation		récent	recent

Il faut protéger les animaux en danger. It is essential to protect endangered animals.
Tout le monde devrait lutter contre la pollution de notre planète. Everyone should fight against the pollution of our planet.
Chez nous, on fait recycler nos bouteilles et nos journaux. At home, we have our bottles and newspapers recycled.

Discuss any part of France you know about

les boules (f)	French bowls		un villageois	villager
une gendarmerie	police station		ça m'est égal	it's all the same to me; I don't care
le gouvernement	government			
un quartier	part of town		étonnant	amazing
une taxe	tax		inadmissible	unacceptable

au milieu de   in the middle of
ce n'est pas la peine   it's not worth it; there's no point

(See also: page 69)

construire   to build
protester   to protest
pourtant   however

Les vieux jouent aux boules sous les arbres sur la place.
Le gouvernement veut construire une autoroute autour de la ville.
Il y aura bientôt une centrale nucléaire.
Les villageois trouvent ça inadmissible.
À mon avis, ce n'est pas la peine de protester.

The old men play bowls under the trees in the square.
The government wants to build a motorway round the town.
There will soon be a nuclear power station there.
The villagers find that unacceptable.
In my opinion, it's not worth protesting.

◀ *Solutions* ▶

Meilleure mémoire 1, page 4
Il y a vingt livres.

Votre score:
Réponse exacte en moins de 30 secondes: Bravo!
Réponse exacte en moins de 40 secondes: C'est bien!
Réponse exacte en plus de 40 secondes: Pas de panique!
Avez-vous travaillé dans le calme et avec la concentration nécessaire?

Meilleure mémoire 2, page 7
Il y a dix-neuf vélos.

Votre score:
Réponse exacte en moins de trente secondes: Bravo!
Réponse exacte en trente secondes: Bien!
Réponse exacte en plus de trente secondes: Continuez à faire ces exercices. Vous pouvez aussi inventer d'autres exercices, par exemple:
• pour développer la mémoire auditive, écoutez la radio et essayez de dire qui parle (on peut faire la même chose au téléphone).
• pour développer votre mémoire visuelle, fermez les yeux et essayez de voir une rue que vous prenez chaque jour ou une pièce chez vous:

où sont les portes, de quelle couleur sont les murs?

Meilleure mémoire 3, page 13
1. un film d'épouvante 2. le petit déjeuner 3. l'Allemagne
4. le Royaume-Uni 5. la salle à manger 6. une brosse à dents
7. un lave-vaisselle 8. un fauteuil 9. confortable 10. la natation

Comptez un point par bonne réponse.

Votre score:
8 à 10: Bravo! 5 à 7: Bien!
0 à 4: Vous pouvez faire encore des progrès avec votre mémoire verbale. Que faire?
C'est facile. Demandez à un(e) ami(e) d'adapter cet exercice et de préparer d'autres listes de mots avec deux lettres absentes. Votre ami(e) peut baser ses listes sur les listes dans ce livre.

Meilleure mémoire 4, page 18
Ce sont toutes des choses qu'on peut manger ou boire. Voici les quatre groupes:

À manger froid   **chaud**
glace au chocolat   croque-

sandwich au fromage
croissant
framboise
radis
ananas

monsieur

frites
hot-dog

À boire froid   **chaud**
coca-cola   thé
jus d'orange   café-
eau minérale   crème
bière
limonade
vin rouge

Meilleure mémoire 5, Page 27
1. un lapin 2. des patins en ligne 3. une montagne
4. un lac 5. une piscine
6. une banque 7. un billet
8. un poisson 9. un stade

Vous êtes content(e) de votre résultat? Sinon, pensez à ce que vous pouvez faire pour faire des progrès.

Meilleure mémoire 6, page 39
1e: C'est la gare SNCF.
2b: C'est l'hôpital.
3a: C'est la poste.
3f: C'est la piscine.
4b: C'est le commissariat de police.
4c: C'est l'hôtel de ville.

Votre score:
4 à 6 réponses correctes: Bravo!
2 ou 3 réponses correctes: Bien!
0 ou 1 réponses correctes: Oh, là, là!

Meilleure mémoire 7, page 43
1. Il est sept heures. 2. Il est quatre heures moins le quart.
3. Il est deux heures vingt.
4. Il est neuf heures moins vingt.
5. Il est dix heures et demie.

Votre score:
4 ou 5 réponses exactes en moins de 4 minutes: Bravo!
3 à 5 réponses exactes en plus de 4 minutes: Bien!
0 à 2 réponses exactes: Oh, là, là!

Meilleure mémoire 8, page 45
un arrêt d'autobus, une bicyclette (un vélo), un train, une voiture (une auto), une usine, une caissière, un journal, un agent de police, une dentiste, un serveur, un facteur, un fermier.

Votre score:
10–12 mots corrects: Bravo!
5–9 mots corrects: Bien!
0–4 mots corrects: Oh, là, là!

Testez-vous activités

page 15: 10 francs 50

page 17: B) Un café et un jus d'orange, s'il vous plaît.

page 20: Cette personne aime les animaux.

page 24: Christmas – Noël

page 31: Prenez la première rue à droite

page 33: 11.30 to 14.00 and Saturdays

page 35: des vêtements pour homme

page 37: It's drinking water

page 40: C) Elles attendent dans le métro.

page 49: Avez-vous une chambre avec douche pour une personne? C'est pour une nuit. Ça coûte combien par nuit?

page 58: Miss 100,000 volts is what prison guards and condemned prisoners call the electric chair in the USA.

page 59:
1. Il commence à 21 heures 10.
2. Du roman de Louis Pergaud, 'La guerre des boutons.'
3. La Terre

page 64:
1. PARC NATIONAL
2. MONTAGNE
3. PÊCHE
4. CAMPING
5. CHEVAL

page 74: We accept:
– only clean clothes in good condition
– only men's shoes
The shop is a charity shop which sells second hand clothes.

page 79: Elle travaille dans une station-service.

page 81: 1-C 2-B 3-A 4-D

page 84: Au bureau de poste.

page 87:
1. Je pourrais aller au bal des sapeurs-pompier.
2. Je pourrais visiter le jardin exotique.
3. À la place du village de Bar-sur-Loup.